Gaia, Christ
and the
Evolution of Humanity

David Spangler

DEDICATION

This book is lovingly dedicated
to the Christ within us each.

Gaia, Christ, And The Evolution Of Humanity

Copyright © 2025 David Spangler and
The Lorian Association

David Spangler has asserted his right to be identified as the author of this work. The Lorian Association has asserted its right to be identified as the copyright owner of this work. All rights are reserved, including the right to reproduce this book, or portions thereof, in any form. Reviewers may quote brief passages. Artificial Intelligence (AI) use of this material is strictly prohibited.

Cover and Interior Design by Jeremy Berg

Published by Lorian Press LLC
Coloma, Michigan

ISBN: 978-1-939790-79-8

Spangler/David
Gaia, Christ, And The Evolution Of Humanity/David Spangler

First Edition: November 2025

Printed in the United States of America
and other countries

www.lorian.org

ACKNOWLEDGMENTS

First, I want to gratefully acknowledge the support and participation of all the subscribers who made *Views from the Borderland* possible.

Second, I wish to acknowledge my good friend of many years, Don Nichol, whose timely suggestion led to the creation of this book.

Finally, I wish to acknowledge the work of my Lorian colleague and friend, Jeremy Berg, who made *Views* possible, and the love, wisdom, and companionship of my wife, Julia, who makes everything possible!

CONTENTS

INTRODUCTION	1
CHAPTER ONE: Issue 17, June 2015	4
CHAPTER TWO: Issue 18, September, 2015	36
CHAPTER THREE: Issue 25, September, 2017	71
CHAPTER FOUR: Issue 26, December 2017	103
CHAPTER 5: Issue 28, June 2018	135
CHAPTER SIX: Issue 31, March, 2019	158
APPENDIX: The Grail Space Exercise	196

INTRODUCTION

For eleven years between 2011 and 2022, I wrote and published a journal in which I could share the results of various esoteric and mystical explorations in which I was engaged. Called *Views from the Borderland,* this journal came out four times a year for subscribers, and each issue was paired with an online forum that ran for a week during which time I would answer questions or engage in discussions prompted by the material covered in that quarter's issue. Eventually, 44 issues were published, along with transcripts of the four yearly forums themselves. All told, this volume of material averaged about 200 to 250 pages per year, the equivalent of a large book, or somewhere in the neighborhood of 3000 pages of original material over the eleven years.

There was no grand master plan behind *Views*; I often didn't know until I actually started writing an issue just what material would be covered. I simply wanted a venue through which I could share with interested others my experiences arising from my engagements with the subtle worlds and my conversations with my subtle colleagues. What I was looking for was conversation and discussion around these topics, and this is what I got.

I was privileged to attract a dedicated group of subscribers, many of whom relished an opportunity to deepen their own explorations and experiences through meaningful conversations with others of like mind. Over the years, a dynamic community developed around the *Views* forums. These were not classes; I was already teaching classes for the Lorian Association. They were more like salons in which I would provide a topic through a particular issue of *Views* and then we would all have at it in the forums, engaging in mutually supportive and respectful conversations. We were all explorers engaged with the terrains of spirit.

The forty-four issues of *Views* are now owned by Lorian as part of its resources and archives; it's material that Lorian and its faculty can draw upon in the future. The transcripts of the forums, however, are protected by a Covenant of Confidentiality that all participants signed. This said simply that nothing people shared in the forums would be available to the public. This was done to create a safe space in which individuals felt free to share their deepest spiritual and psychic experiences with each other without fearing that their vulnerability would show up without their permission somewhere on the Internet.

Although each issue was like a separate report from my own explorations—what I called my "field notes"—there were certain themes that I often came back to because they were central to my own inner spiritual work. One of these themes was Gaia and the emergence of the Gaian Human as a next step in humanity's spiritual evolution. Recently, a good friend of mine, Don Nichol, who had been a *Views* subscriber from the beginning, asked if I could collect together and edit into a book all the material that I had written in *Views* concerning Gaia, the Christ, and humanity's evolutionary journey.

That is what this book is about.

You will note from the Table of Contents that the issues of *Views* presented here are not necessarily sequential. Sometimes a year or more may pass between one issue and another as I would address a theme, such as Gaia, and then not discuss it again for several months. Thus, the material in this book is organized thematically, not by date.

As you will see in reading what follows, I regularly work with non-physical or "subtle" individuals, largely with a set of ideas, principles, and practices I call Incarnational

Spirituality. Most of the subscribers to *Views* were students of Incarnational Spirituality; thus, its concepts, principles, and practices were familiar to them. If you are coming to Incarnational Spirituality for the first time and wonder about some of the ideas and terms I use in these journals, may I recommend you read the following books. *Apprenticed to Spirit* will introduce you to who I am and the nature of my training and work, and *Journey into Fire* will give you a basic introduction to Incarnational Spirituality (or IS) itself. Other books by Lorian Press LLC authored by me or about IS can be found by going to the Lorian website at Lorian.org.

At the beginning of each issue of *Views*, I offered the following caveat:

All the material contained in this journal is based on my personal observations and experiences. While I present it as accurately and clearly as I am able, it is subject to the limitations of my own background, understanding, bias, perceptual abilities, and skills of interpretation. While I have years of experience in this area, I am most certainly not infallible. I am still exploring and learning. This being said, I invite you to join with me in this exploration. If anything you read here resonates with your mind and heart, may it be a blessing and a help to you.

This holds true for the material in this book.

David Spangler
September, 2025

CHAPTER ONE
Issue 17, June 2015

This issue we turn our attention to Gaia. This is the name James Lovelock gave to the Earth as an organism, and it's also the name that the ancient Greeks gave to the goddess of Nature and of the world. In the esoteric traditions, the planet is also seen as a living, spiritual being, and Gaia is one of the names given to this Planetary Spirit or World Soul. Partnering with Gaia is one of the key ideas of Incarnational Spirituality, for our incarnations are influenced by and also influence the incarnation of Gaia as a whole. How we might do this is the theme for this issue as I present a project that is my current line of exploration and experimentation.

A Changing of the Guard

For some months now, what I call my "Pit Crew"—the non-physical beings who are my usual and closest inner colleagues—has been changing, with some individuals moving into the background or leaving altogether and new individuals coming forward. I knew there was a reason for this as I had been sensing for some time a change in my work. However, the exact nature of this change has not always been clear. As happens sometimes in our lives, I felt myself caught in the "betwixt-and-between", no longer part of an older flow of energy and work but not yet part of what was unfolding.

Over the years, all the inner beings I've worked with, from my mentor John back in the Sixties and Seventies right up to the present time, have all said that the "Great Work" of our time is to understand the interconnected nature of all life and as a result, to foster and create wholeness in the world. They have spoken at times as well of an "initiation" which the Spirit of the planet itself is going through, one creating changes at all levels of life so that new states of integration and wholeness may be achieved. However, while acknowledging this larger context, the work on which I and my inner colleagues have been collaborating through the medium of Incarnational Spirituality has been focused on the individual, especially over the last decade.

With the arrival of this new set of colleagues and partners, I can tell the emphasis is shifting. The individual is still important as a sovereign, generative source of spiritual Light and creativity, but more and more the focus is shifting towards a planetary context. The work ahead is one of understanding Gaia on many levels and learning to partner with greater awareness and skill with this Planetary Spirit. Consequently, this has been a focal point for my research of late and for my most recent contacts with my newer subtle colleagues.

A Functional Approach

Thinking about what "partnering with Gaia" meant and how to go about it, I thought of an approach that I've used successfully with various subtle beings and have written about in classes. Essentially, it's based on understanding the functions or tasks with which a being is engaged. By aligning with the spirit of such a function or task, particular through love, a state of resonance is created. For instance, if I want to attune to a nature spirit in the garden, I ask myself what it is this spirit is seeking to do; what is its function? I may not know or understand all of its functions, but at the least, I assume it is trying to bring love and vital energies to the plants under its care. So how can I do the same? If I make myself a conduit of love and vitality to my garden, then I'm sharing the function of the nature spirit, which builds a resonance between us.

It's no different in principle than making friends with someone by learning to share that person's interests. If two people are interested in the same things or especially if they are doing the same things, there's a natural affinity between them.

So the question becomes, what are Gaia's functions? What is the task of the Planetary Spirit?

Gaia's Body

Years ago in several of my classes, I included a discussion on "thinking like a planet". At the time, it wasn't an attempt to get into the mind of the Planetary Spirit so much as it was a way of talking about systems thinking and ecological awareness. The idea was that Gaia was a complex system of interconnected and interdependent lives, and that Gaian thought supported and integrated that complexity. To "think like a planet" used Gaia as a metaphor for the kind of holistic and integrative thinking that creates wholeness, a kind of thinking much needed in our world today.

However, thinking like a planet is much more than a metaphor. As my inner colleagues have said on more than one occasion, the souls of humanity originally came to this world not only to offer service to Gaia's incarnational process but also to learn what it meant to embody, if only on a personal scale, the creative thought, love, and fostering of life that is a hallmark of our Planetary Spirit. In other words, we really are here to learn how to think like a planet.

NOTE: *Although I didn't emphasize it at the time I wrote this in 2015, "thinking" to me means more than a cognitive or intellectual activity—more than just forming thoughts about something. It means a form of apprehension or perception of a reality emerging* *from a felt sense of wholeness. It means experiencing in a full-body way. A traditional mystical way of saying this is "thinking with the heart," but in Incarnational Spirituality, I prefer to think of it as thinking from Presence, where Presence is a spirit of wholeness within us. Actually, I coined a word to describe this:* holopoiesis, *the impulse to perceive and create connections and wholeness. "Thinking," to me, is a holopoietic activity that simultaneously sees the difference between the seer and the seen and also experiences their interconnectedness and wholeness. Such thinking by its nature gives rise to love as an act of perception and connectedness. To think like a planet, then, is to think from an awareness of the interconnectedness and wholeness that creates the world as a unity able to manifest diversity. —Sept. 2025.*

However, there is more to thinking like a planet than just thinking ecologically, however important that may be. As a way of pursuing the kind of attunement through shared resonance that I mentioned above, I wanted to think just what Gaia's functions might be. Again, this is more than metaphor. What we think of as the subtle worlds are really aspects of Gaia's subtle body, and this body or field of living energy has its own metabolism. For instance, the movement of human souls from the soul realms to the physical plane and back again provides a kind of circulation through which subtle energies originating at a higher frequency of life are able to flow into the earth through the incarnational process and, via the Post-Mortem Realms, return to the higher frequencies again. This is an automatic process—it happens whether we are aware of it or not—but we can become conscious of it and even more, we can empower this circulation through our mental, emotional, and physical actions, heightening the process.

There are other currents and activities that are part of

Gaia's subtle field, some of which impact life at a physical or incarnate level and some of which don't. In my own experience, some—perhaps many—of these currents and flows of living energy are mediated in some manner by beings who are adapted for that purpose or who choose to be a medium or carrier for a particular subtle energy. The equivalent in our body would be red blood cells adapted to carry oxygen and nutrients to other cells, or, for that matter, the muscle and endothelial cells that form the arteries, veins and capillaries along which our blood flows.

Thinking about this, I drew a picture illustrating some of the functions that I'm aware of or have encountered. There are undoubtedly others that I'm not aware of, and probably wouldn't understand if I were, but here are seven that stand out for me.

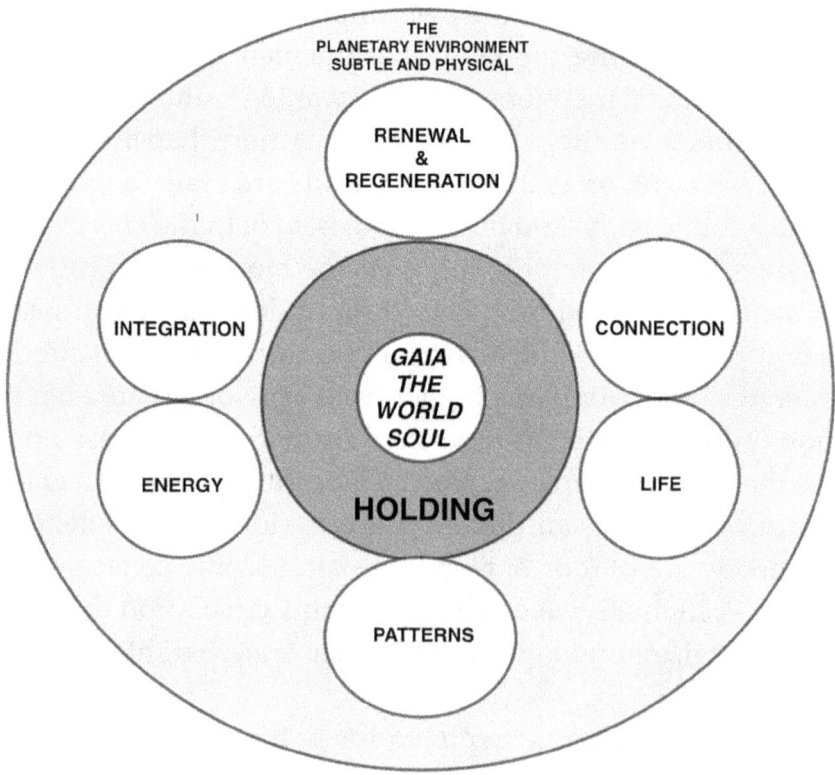

This picture represents a relationship between functions, not between "planes" or "levels of being". Each of the circles holds one or more activities that in a sense functions like an "organ" of Gaian physiology. What is not clearly shown in this two-dimensional image is how these activities interrelate and interpenetrate each other to manifest as a whole organism. I have to leave that up to your imaginations as drawing it is beyond my skills.

So what do these circles or "organs" represent?

First, there is Gaia itself, the actual Planetary Spirit or Soul-Being with its own unique Identity. This is the Intelligence and Beingness that is holding and infusing the planet Earth with its presence to make it a place where life can form and evolve in a myriad of ways. It is also evolving in relationship to its own capacities and to its surrounding cosmic and sacred environment. In this, it is not so different from you and me, though the scale and complexity of its activity and evolution is obviously beyond anything we experience as human beings. I have pictured this as the central organizing force, but in fact, the presence and Identity of Gaia permeate all the activities and structures that make up the world.

Surrounding Gaia at the center is a circle with the word "Holding." This represents one of the fundamental activities of Gaia: the capacity to create, sustain and nurture a "space" or condition that allows all the various functions, activities, levels, aspects, and beings that make up the totality of the world to gather, co-exist and work together. It is holding a space for evolution, experimentation, growth, and unfoldment. It is this basic function that makes possible all the others.

The rest of the circles are not meant to wholly define all the activities of Gaia. They merely represent those activities and functions which I have personally encountered in my investigations into the subtle worlds; I'm sure there are other functions of which I have no knowledge or understanding and thus which are not pictured here. I'm not trying to draw an accurate inner anatomy of Gaia; I'm only suggesting a way of thinking about the Planetary Spirit that focuses on its activities.

First, I'm aware of an activity which at the planetary level deals with the creation and expression of organizing and structuring patterns. I might think of this as the "imaginative function" of Gaia. Some of these patterns Gaia perceives and takes on from its own cosmic environment, but others it is generating on its own. These living patterns shape, regulate, stimulate, and influence the flow of energy and the manifestation of life here on Earth. For instance, there is a pattern (or perhaps a set of interrelated patterns) that is responsible for the development of humanity and that holds the image of the Ideal or Sacred Human towards the expression of which our species is evolving.

Over the years, I've been aware of vast beings whom I think of as planetary angels or archangels and Devas. Their activity deals with the planet as a whole and its relationship to solar and stellar influences and energies. They work in close proximity to the consciousness of Gaia and partner with it in the creation of the patterns and "laws" that drive planetary life and evolution.

This function, though, like all the others I discuss here, is not confined to a "higher level" but permeates the world to empower and influence the pattern-making capacities of all forms of life. It is present in us as our function of imagination. It's not that Gaia imagines through us (though with proper attunement to the World Soul, this is certainly possible) but that our power to imagine and create patterns and images to shape and guide our lives reflects and is empowered by the equivalent function within Gaia. After all, our incarnate minds emerge from the union of our soul with the World Soul and thus reflect the powers and functions inherent within both, just as children reflect the genetic patterns of both their father and their mother.

Another circle I've labeled as "Life" and metaphorically, I could say it represents the heart activity of Gaia. While all life ultimately emerges from the Sacred, planetary life--whether physical or subtle, organic or inorganic—is formed largely out of Gaia's energetic substance, participates in the planetary "life-field", and is fed by the life energies that Gaia generates. These Gaian life-energies, as well as other vital and stimulating forces received from solar and stellar sources, circulate through the entire subtle and physical bodies of Gaia, propelled by this "Life" or "Heart" function.

Whereas in our bodies, circulation takes place within veins, arteries, and capillaries, for Gaia, it is living beings, including ourselves, who are the instruments of this circulation of living, vital energies, or, conversely, the cause of its obstruction. Such beings include those we call angels, Devas and nature spirits.

Two of the circles represent related functions which I call Connection and Integration. The former represents all those energies and activities that promote and sustain interconnections between all the elements that make up Gaia's life. The latter in turns draws all these connections into an integrated coherency that permits Gaia to function as a whole system. It also includes, I believe, those functions that in our bodies would be activities of digestion and assimilation. In Gaia, this occurs through the activity of a wide variety of beings—and ultimately in one form or another within all beings upon and within the earth. Where this function fails or is not properly attended to, obstruction and toxicity can result.

The activity I've labeled "Regeneration and Renewal" is akin to the function of the liver and kidneys and to some extent that of the immune system in our bodies (though again, we have to be careful about drawing the parallels too closely between Gaia as a being of spirit and energy and ourselves as physical entities). This is a vital function that partly involves cleansing, healing, repairing, and regenerating connections and energy flows that have become broken or obstructed. But it's also about keeping things "fresh", so to speak, attuned to the renewing spirit of the Sacred. In the Christian tradition, this function brings the presence and power of Grace into the life of Gaia and all within the planet. Particularly for those lives that operate within the incarnate realms and are subject to time and space, this function offers freedom from bondage to habit. It expresses forgiveness. It is a "de-cluttering" function, removing what is no longer needed and vivifying what is still important or is emerging.

The outermost part of the picture represents the "Fields of Expression" which (very loosely) might be imagined as Gaia's musculature, the instruments of action. These are the activities and manifestations of all the beings, subtle and physical, that live as part of the Earth, pursuing their own courses of evolution and development while contributing to the overall expression of Gaia as a planet.

Listing these functions isn't simply a philosophical or mental exercise. As I've said at other times, I experience the subtle environment—the non-physical counterpart to the physical environment in which I am immediately located—as having fluid characteristics. It's a bit like being underwater in that I'm aware of currents that flow through this environment carrying different qualities and impacting my own subtle bodies in different ways. There really isn't a good way to describe this using physical metaphors. Each of these currents has a "flavor" or a "feel" to it. It has a living identity. But the currents that carry vitality and life are different from those that promote connections or that act to cleanse and renew an area. Others might experience them differently, but this is how I experience them.

The range of energies and "currents" I feel can be quite large, and they have different "frequencies" in that they can co-exist in the same space but not necessarily interact. In this they are akin to all the television and radio shows that exist around us in space but which we need a TV or radio to detect; even then, I have to set my TV to a different channel to receive the informational current coming from our local CBS station than I do to receive the broadcast from the local ABC station. Although both waves of energy occupy the same space in my living room, they are on different frequencies.

Thus it's possible to attune my consciousness in one way and feel the living energies coming from the spirit of nearby Lake Sammamish whereas I need to attune in a different way to feel the currents coming from Mt. Rainer about fifty miles to the south. But I'm aware generally that both are present in my subtle environment, along with a lot of other energies coming from a wide variety of human and non-human sources.

However, the "currents" stirred up by and representing the activity of the Gaian functions I've listed are different in feel, when I'm able to feel them. It's more often that I feel their effects than that I feel the "functions" themselves, much like I know a wind is blowing over Lake Washington when I see the waves it creates in the water.

My point is that these functions are not philosophical ideas but objective energetic or spiritual activities initiated by the life and consciousness of the Planetary Spirit. What is even more important and exciting about this is that all these functions, including the basic one of Holding, are not confined to any location within Gaia. The scale, intensity and expression of a particular function may differ from one level of life within Gaia to another, but the actual function pervades the whole of Gaia's being and may be expressed by any life within Gaia. You and I each embody all these Gaian functions within the scale and boundaries of our human lives. In holographic fashion, the parts really do contain the whole. Gaia is enfolded and embedded in us as fully as we are embedded in Gaia.

In fact, it is highly likely that the functions I perceive and that I've listed are simply those that I can recognize precisely because they are akin to spiritual and energetic functions within me as an incarnate human being. The maple tree in my backyard, not to mention the crows that often sit in its branches, might experience quite different functions or the same functions in different ways. When it comes to "as above, so below", it's not always easy to know which side is reflecting which. But even if I'm only recognizing the functions that I as a human being am structured to recognize and understand, these functions are not projections. They still exist as Gaian activities of some nature, and as such I can align with them and participate in them.

Participating in Gaia

How might we go about engaging and participating with Gaia's field of living energies? In one sense, there's nothing we need to do because we are already participating in this field. Whatever qualities or subtle energies we radiate into our surrounding environment become part of Gaia's subtle body for better or worse. As long as we are alive in this world, we can't *not* be part of Gaia. We are like fish in the ocean; Gaia's life and energy form the sea in which we are swimming.

Beyond this, there are two ways we can act as participants in Gaia. One way is to use our equivalent of the Gaian functions—our capacities to imagine, to radiate vitality and life, to create connections and to integrate them into a larger wholeness, to regenerate and renew, and to hold—in our everyday lives as acts intended to benefit the world around us. Gaia is all about nourishing and supporting life and development. I can nourish and support life as well.

Likewise, I can act toward the lives and objects around me in loving ways that bring blessing to them as best and as appropriately as I can. When I do, I am giving something to the world. I'm loving and blessing Gaia and helping its incarnational well-being.

Energy hygiene and subtle activism both fall into this category of ways to assist the energy conditions of the world using the resources of our own individual energy fields. When we do so, we are helping not only particular individuals, beings, and situations but also Gaia itself.

In other words, I can use the spiritual and energetic capacities I have as an incarnate human being to make the environments and lives around me—all of which are part of Gaia—better than they were before. This is an important form of participation.

But there's a second way, and that is to become an energetic conduit for the functions of Gaia, to align with them and to allow them to work through me. In this way, I shift from acting toward Gaia or upon Gaia to actually being Gaia in a functional way, though on a human scale.

There will come a time when humanity will know the reality of Gaia and will participate in its life and partner with its intents and functions as naturally and organically as we now perceive and work with the physical environment around us. When this will happen, I do not know, but for anyone willing to do some exploration and work, he or she doesn't have to wait for that time. A Gaian consciousness and field of energy is available for us to develop now.

The Personal Gaian Field

Years ago I wrote about learning to "think like a planet". What I meant by this at the time was learning to think ecologically and holistically and to be aware of the interconnectedness and interdependency of life. It was essentially a metaphor for thinking in terms of whole systems and their interactions. I also wrote then that to "act like a planet" was to act with love to support and empower life around us.

But there's a deeper possibility here and that is to enter into the stream of thinking, loving, and acting that make up the life of Gaia itself and to participate in the expression of Gaia's "functions". In so doing, I become a "muscle" of the planet. The way I've been exploring this is to consider the development of what could be called our "personal Gaian field".

Here's a picture:

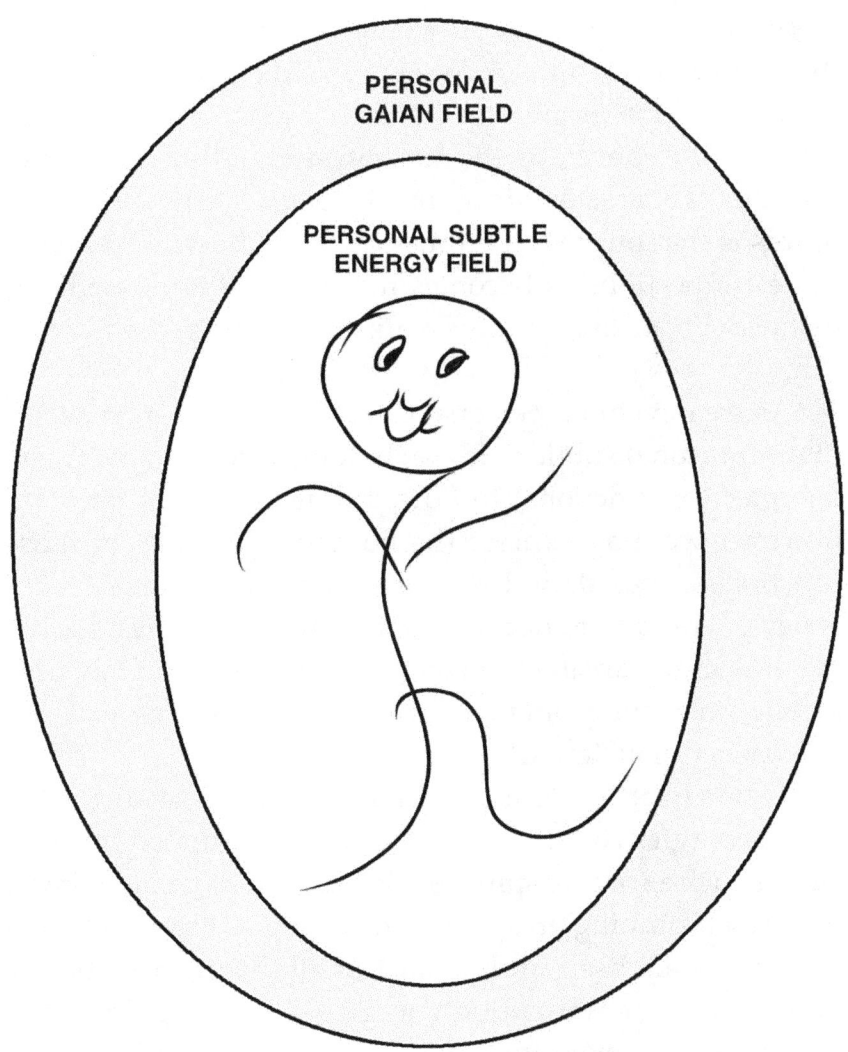

This "Personal Gaian Field is really an expanded or extended version of our personal subtle field, or I might say, a form of attunement that gives our personal subtle field the capacity to work directly with Gaian energies. I've drawn this as two concentric circles in order to show that they are two different things, but this reflects the limitations of my artistic skill rather than any accurate representation of how these two fields interact. It would be more accurate to say that the texture of our subtle energy field changes as we take on and become attuned to Gaian energies. The "Personal Gaian Field" develops the capacity to hold the quality of love that is characteristic of the Planetary Spirit. One result of this is that our field becomes open to and vitalized with more connections; it becomes more naturally holopoietic, instinctively or organically creating wholeness as fully as it can.

As we develop a personal Gaian field or a Gaian aspect of our personal subtle field, we become a conduit for Gaian energies (or functions) to flow through us, in addition to however we may express the human equivalent of those functions in our daily lives. In a way, we become "mini-Gaias". We radiate not only our own Self-Light and other subtle energies arising from our natural activities of thinking, feeling, and acting, but in a way, we radiate Gaia as well. We become a Gaian "muscle".

Trying to attune to the Gaian field directly (as distinct to Gaian energies coming through or being mediated by other beings such as nature spirits or Devas) proved challenging. I felt myself running up against a dead end as I couldn't seem to "find" Gaia itself in the midst of all the other planetary and environmental subtle energies. At this point, after several days of experimentation and unsuccessful attempts at attuning to Gaia, I got some help from one of my inner colleagues, a being I call Phillip. Here is what he had to say.

> PHILLIP: As you explore participating in the life and energy field of Gaia, let me offer some observations and suggestions from my side of life. At your incarnate level of life, the Planetary Soul is a diffused presence. You are assuredly part of its living field of being, but this field

attenuates and changes in character as it moves into the physical world. Think of making a soup from chicken broth. The broth serves as the medium in which other items, such as various vegetables and spices, are blended. The soup will have a character of its own depending on what is in it, and it may be that the flavor of the chicken broth itself will be faint in the final product. Yet it is there and can be detected by a sensitive palate.

The chicken broth is a distillation of the chicken and carries some of its qualities, but there is a great difference between a chicken and the broth that comes from it. You would not mistake one for the other! Gaia is like the chicken, and its field of energy is like the broth, a distillation of its qualities. At your level of life, you deal with the broth, and even then, as with the soup, the flavor of the broth may be hard to detect because of all the other flavors—all the other life-forces and energies—that are present.

I say this because Gaia as a being is not easily accessible from your level of life, though its field is. The attenuation of its field is purposeful just as using chicken broth as the base for a soup is purposeful, and for similar reasons. The broth carries other ingredients and provides a medium for their qualities and flavors—their identities—to emerge and be known, as well as to be connected and blended together in the identity of the soup itself. If the broth remained a chicken, solid and with its own distinct shape, soup would not be possible. Your would just have a collection of ingredients, not the wholeness of the soup.

Gaia's field, like the broth, allows many forms of life and consciousness to be held—and connected together—in ways that allow their unique identities and qualities to emerge as well. You can be fully human because Gaia is not being fully Gaia in a way that would leave no room for your soul identity and your humanity to manifest. You are part of a soup of which Gaia is the broth.

Yet there *is* a chicken. Gaia does exist as an actual being, but its "native" domain, so to speak, is many levels of vibration and life removed from you. Even what constitutes the native level of your soul is not the same as where Gaia exists as the "chicken". The "pressure" or density of the Light, the love, the complexity of connections and consciousness in Gaia's native state is very hard for a human soul to sustain at your current level of collective evolution, though there are advanced members of our species who can, for short times at least, enter into the full presence of the Planetary Spirit.

In a sense, then, there are two "Gaias" who metaphorically may be thought of as the "chicken" and the "broth". It is really the latter that you experience as the planetary field that supports and empowers life. For one of the functions of Gaia is to make soup, and humanity is one of the ingredients. To do this, broth is needed. This broth is thickest and most concentrated closest to the Planetary Spirit and thinnest and most attenuated in the incarnate realms that you inhabit where particularity and boundaries and the experiences they offer are important. Understand that even with this attenuation of the field, the "broth of Gaia" is still rich with power and flavor. But it is designed to allow other flavors, other identities, to come to the fore in order to know themselves.

Let me boldly push this metaphor further. One function of the broth in the making of a soup is to hold and distribute the heat that cooks the ingredients, releasing their qualities and flavors into the whole. Without the broth, you have a pile of vegetables in a pot which, if you apply heat, will not produce soup but burned vegetables. The broth allows each ingredient to receive the heat—the energy—it needs to allow it to release it flavors.

This is precisely what the Gaian field—the Gaian broth—does. It is a medium through which the energy of life, of Light, and of love may be distributed to all the lives evolving within the planetary field in a manner that they can receive and not be burnt. We are all being "cooked", you see, absorbing energies that allow each of us in our own way to evolve, unfold, develop, and release the divine potentials, the "flavors" within us. Gaia is not necessarily the source of those energies—they come from many sources, Gaia included—but Gaia is the medium through which they are received and distributed, just as the broth receives the heat from the stove and distributes it throughout the soup as it cooks.

So what is the role of the incarnate human individual in the Gaian soup?

Well, you can certainly contribute your flavors—your love, your Self-Light, your life-affirming energies and actions, the gifts of your unique identity. You can be a vegetable in the broth, putting forth its vegetable goodness! But can you be the broth itself?

Here we touch into the mystery of how the whole lives within the part and vice versa, the mystery of the fractal nature of existence. For the answer is, yes, indeed you can be broth as well. You do this by finding the broth-like qualities in yourselves and adding them to the Gaian broth around you. You can enhance the capacities of the Gaian broth, enabling it to do its work as a broth even better. And what does the broth do? It will contribute its flavor to the soup, but depending on the soup and the other ingredients, this may not be its greatest contribution. What the broth provides is a medium in which individual identities may gather, offer their unique qualities and work together to create something none could have done on its own. The broth holds. The broth connects. The broth makes collaboration and emergence possible.

I will abandon this metaphor now for it has gone as far as it can go. Let me speak more directly. The field of Gaia is "thin" where you live in the incarnate world, and deliberately so. It still holds, connects, energizes, empowers, and distributes nurturing and qualities, but it does so in a "thinner", less obtrusive way than you would find closer to the Being that is the Planetary Spirit. However, if you attune to this field, you can "thicken" it, so to speak. You can make the Gaian field more effective in your incarnate environment, allowing the intent of the Planetary Spirit to manifest more clearly.

You can by your attention, presence, and attunement, heighten the Gaian intent—the purpose of the "broth"—and enhance the capacities to hold, to connect, and to empower. One of your exercises, the Grail Space, already moves in this direction. By aligning your energy field with that of Gaia and creating Grail Space from that alignment, you can "thicken" the Gaian field within the circle and the chalice you create. I will leave you to work out the details.

However, I would add two pieces of advice. First, the field of Gaia is not easy to discern at your level of life. It is like the proverbial still, small voice in the midst of many loud voices. It is its function to minimize its identity so that other identities may come forward in their evolution. The energy fields that are most accessible to you are those produced by other beings who share the earth with you. For instance, you will discern more easily the energy of your maple tree or of the spirit of the lake near your home or the energy of the mountains that surround you. To find Gaia in their midst requires subtlety of attention and patience.

Of course, you can attune to Gaia *through* the life of other organisms in nature, such as your maple tree, for example, with this organism acting as an intermediary between you and the Planetary Spirit, but this is different from blending with the Gaian field directly. Also, when you do this, you connect with Gaia through the medium of another being and its relationship with the planetary field. This may be different from the relationship you have, so when possible, finding your own innate connection is preferable.

The challenge is that at your level, Gaia is a non-local, non-specific field of life that holds all other lives; it is like attuning to the air around you on a still, clear, peaceful day when not a single breeze is stirring to tell you of the air's presence. You can do it, but you must ensure your attention is not drawn to other things in the environment.

You might begin by attuning to your own life—not to your identity or to the content of your autobiography and not even to your body and its metabolism, but to life itself as it animates and energizes your being. For Gaia is a presence of life. If you attune to your own presence of life, it may be a portal into the field of planetary life that surrounds you just as paying attention to your breath can enhance your awareness of the air around you. Experiment! See what you can discover.

Blessings as always!

Experimenting

With Phillip's encouragement, it was time for some experimenting. For any work with subtle dimensions and forces, I always start by affirming my Sovereignty and by filling my heart with love. I always want to engage the life around me, whether physical or subtle, from a loving and honoring place.

As I go through my day, unless I pay attention otherwise, I probably see the environment around me much the way everyone else does as a collection of physical objects and structures and living creatures, in other words, a blend of the organic and the inorganic. If I pay attention, though, then I'm aware that everything around me is an expression of life in some manner; everything radiates a living energy. It's then that I acknowledge that I am a fish in a sea of life, the same as everyone and everything else. If Gaia is a presence of life, as Phillip said, then this is the attitude and awareness I want to have to experiment with attuning to the Planetary Spirit.

So I was "standing in Sovereignty" as the phrase goes in Incarnational Spirituality and expanding my awareness in a loving way into the sense of life around me…and this is when the challenges began.

The first challenge, as Phillip had warned me, was that it was easier to attune to the "veggies", to use his metaphor, than it was to the "broth". Just when I thought I was attuning to Gaia, I realized as I went deeper into the felt sense of that attunement that it was another source. For example, I found myself picking up on the energy radiating from the land, that is to say, from the ecosystem that makes up Puget Sound with its lakes, the Sound itself as a large inlet coming off the Pacific Ocean, and the surrounding mountains, most of which are dormant volcanoes. In one sense, of course, all of this *is* Gaia, or at least a part of Gaia. But it wasn't that to which I wished to attune.

Moving past this, I consistently found myself attuning to a presence which under any other circumstances I would easily and naturally assume was Gaia. This presence was like

"Mother Nature", a Being I could with no difficulty imagine as a great, feminine, goddess-like entity whose loving mantle surrounded the earth. But this, too, I felt wasn't really Gaia but yet another intermediate form.

Part of the challenge was that I have mental images of who and what Gaia is and as a consequence, an expectation of what I should be attuning to and what that contact might be like. These images have grown in me out of a variety of sources: things I've read, myths and narratives I've encountered, other peoples' experiences with Gaia, past inner contacts I've had with Gaian energies, and so on. More to the point, I realized that how I think of Gaia is rooted in my experience of being a human being. For instance, I grew up nurtured by a mother and father, and it's easy to project that felt sense of nourishment and of being parented onto the Planetary Spirit. But is this really what Gaia is, or am I formulating my sense of it based on my emotional nature and whatever needs I might have for being nourished?

After some days of trying, I realized that I wasn't really getting to "the broth" of which Phillip spoke, or if I was, I wasn't recognizing it as such. To use his metaphor, I felt that I was attuning to "*chicken* broth" when I actually needed to attune to the function of *"broth."* I was putting too much attention on the *identity* of Gaia rather than on the *action* or the *doing* of Gaia, if this makes sense. In making a soup, what is required is a liquid, and whether it's chicken broth, beef broth, or vegetable broth makes no difference to the function of the liquid itself in the cooking of the soup (though obviously it will make a lot of difference in terms of flavor, nutrition, and whether it's a soup suitable for vegetarians!).

It wasn't all failure. There were moments of touching into something when I felt "Ah, this is it!" Such moments came when I was able to attune to the "broth-like" action of

Holding. I realized, though, that this sense of holding had to be entirely neutral. In thinking about "being Gaia", I had to be careful not to interpret this to mean being a particular identity but rather on being an action. I wasn't Holding to achieve a particular effect or outcome. I had to step outside any human preconceptions or expectations about what Gaia is or does and just maintain an inner silence that opened in a neutral way to the flow of life. When I was able to do this, I felt that I entered into the Gaian field I was seeking, at least for a moment.

And The Purpose Is...?

In a scientific experiment, when things aren't going quite as expected, it's useful to go back and examine the original question that the experiment is intended to answer. So when I would come up against a blank wall, I would ask, "Why am I doing this?" Even when I felt successful in touching into a Gaian field, it wasn't always clear what the result was or what, if anything, transpired.

To bring more clarity into the process, I would review what had led me into this exploration in the first place. It was really two things. One was a desire to serve. Human beings, for all our challenges and often shoddy behavior towards each other and towards the world, are a complex and advanced consciousness with numerous spiritual capacities that many other species on earth lack. We have an ability to help other, less developed forms of life in their spiritual development. And we also have a capacity to partner with the Planetary Spirit in so doing. I wished to understand more how we can do this.

The other factor in inspiring this exploration is that there are dimensions to our humanity that Gaia can teach us. This teaching isn't through words or concepts. It's by enriching and in some ways altering the structure of our own subtle fields. Looking at this through the eyes of a biologist, I would say that Gaia can modify our subtle metabolism so that we process subtle energies differently. The nature of perception and consciousness themselves changes, becoming more holopoietic. Associating with Gaian energies or the Gaian presence directly seemed to me a way of enhancing this inner transformation and evolution.

So the basic purpose is to see if we as human beings can encounter and embody Gaia directly in a way that enhances our ability to serve and empower other lives around us and also enables us to develop a "richer" or more deeply textured subtle field, a "Gaian-type" subtle field. The possession of such a subtle field, it seems to me, is vital to our ability as a species to adapt to the holistic needs of the planet in the decades and centuries ahead.

An Inner Colleague

When I do this kind of inner research and exploration, my inner colleagues generally want me to go as far as I can on my own before they'll make suggestions, offer to help, or make commentary. If I do find myself blocked and stuck, they like to see if I can make my own way out. But if I'm really stuck, then they will offer help, if only to point out a turning or a path I might have missed.

As I continued with the exploration, my inner colleagues must have decided I'd done enough to warrant another conversation, probably to keep me from going too far afield in a less-than-productive direction. This time it wasn't Philip but another individual for whom I have no name as yet. (Well, this isn't exactly true. All my inner colleagues have names, just not ones that translate easily into words. I know each of them by their "soul note" which is a vibratory signature that my subtle field recognizes, one which is unique to their individual identity.) So, I'll just call him I.C. for "inner colleague".

I.C.: Greetings. In your work with the Planetary Spirit, here are some factors to keep in mind. The first is to remember that you are dealing with subtle realities here where the boundaries are not as distinct or binding as those familiar to you in the physical world. Thus, it is not always easy for you to discern where the energy field of one being ends and that of Gaia begins or vice versa. Conditions are permeable and identities may be shared up to a point.

I say this because there is a planetary Angel or Deva who overlights all living organisms on the earth and is the true inner source for the conception of "Mother Nature" on the one hand or of an Earth Goddess on the other. This being is not Gaia, the Planetary Spirit, but it *is* the World Mother and as such fulfills the mythic role often projected upon Gaia. As our colleague Phillip has said, it is not easy for incarnate human consciousness to discern the Planetary Spirit itself, but it is well within the scope of human capacities to discern and interact with the World Mother. Consequently, it is she who often answers to the designation "Gaia".

But that to which you are seeking to attune is a different order of being altogether, neither Angel nor Deva but a Planetary Spirit. Its role towards life and towards the Earth is different from that of the World Mother or the planetary Angel or Deva. It is an integral part of the energetic body of the Solar Logos, for whom the solar system is its instrument of incarnation and service, and part of an evolving cosmic form as well. So when you attune to

Gaia, you are seeking to attune to a presence that belongs to an environment beyond that of this planet, which is not true to the same degree of the World Mother whose life is the life of the biosphere.

This is one reason for the difficulty you experience. You are not always calibrating your attunement properly, resulting in a connection with the World Mother but not with Gaia. But when you do connect to Gaia, you may not recognize it as such because you may not feel the vibratory signature of the Earth, that is to say, of the land and of the biosphere. You do not feel the presence of life that you expect, is this not so? [*I allowed as to how this was exactly right.—David*]

You feel life, but it is the life that flows through the stellar and solar pathways, which can seem inaccessibly abstract and neutral, as if there is nothing there at all. But it is there; you simply have to adjust your expectations and your direction of attunement. Think of attuning to a presence that is more than the earth, and we feel you will have greater success.

Another factor is that you have the object in mind of partnering with Gaia. You can certainly partner with the World Mother, adding your human energies to hers in a blessing of life, but partnering with Gaia is a different proposition. You have correctly discerned that it requires a neutrality of approach that is not easy to maintain. This is because, to use Phillip's metaphor, you are innately intended to be a vegetable in the soup, not the broth itself. So it is what you offer from your humanness that is important.

But you can appreciate the broth and yes, you can attune to it which, again as Phillip stated, can heighten its holding presence in the environment in which you are performing this attunement. This is no small thing to accomplish, but frankly, it is not your role as a human being to be Gaia in this way. It demands a neutrality of you which at this point in your evolution at least can diminish your human contribution to the whole. This is because at the incarnate level, the Planetary Spirit does not operate as a being but as a field. For you to become that field, you have to set aside your own quality of being a being. You must become more diffuse than is proper for you as a human individuality. There may be situations that provide an exception to this, but this is generally true.

However, there is a good reason to pursue this attunement and the integration of Gaian qualities and pathways of energy within your subtle body. You can certainly become "Gaia-like", and this will enhance your capacity to serve life, much as you surmise.

There is another reason, though, for this attunement. There are a few species in the world in all three kingdoms of the mineral, the vegetative, and the animal that have an innate capacity to receive and process qualities of subtle energy originating in solar and stellar sources. Put another way, these species, and humanity is one of them, can participate in the extra-planetary life of Gaia, though each species will do so in its own unique manner.

There are potentials within your subtle energy field that can be awakened and brought "on-line", so to speak, through an alignment with Gaia's energy field. Your vision of a Gaian field within the individual is accurate, but its purpose is not to passively be a conduit for Gaian functions. Its purpose, when awakened, is to enable you to participate across a wider and deeper spectrum of Gaia's life, which cannot help but enhance your capacities to serve, as well as your ability to partner with the World Mother and other planetary angels and Devas working under her direction.

It is also true that, to use a limited but hopefully useful physical metaphor, the subtle field of the world is itself undergoing a process of "re-wiring". When you attune to Gaia as the Planetary Spirit, you open yourself to this same process within yourself, a case of the macrocosm being reflected in the microcosm. It is no mere metaphor that humanity is in the process of developing a new subtle body. The work you and your colleagues are doing has always been part of this larger planetary project.

More than this I cannot say, but as Phillip has done, I encourage you to experiment and explore.

Blessings!

Where Things Stand

So this is where things stand as of this writing. This is very much a project of research and exploration that is incomplete and ongoing. I'm sure I will have more to share about it in future issues of this Journal. It's one reason I'm stepping out of the kind of teaching I've been doing for the past fifteen years in order to have more time to give to this project.

Although my "field notes" are incomplete, I felt it worthwhile to share this process with you as an example of what one kind of working with the Borderlands can be like. There is nothing cut and dried about this process. I had thought at one point I would have exercises to offer that would help you experience an attunement to Gaia and to your own Gaian field, but I'm nowhere near being able to articulate yet just what those exercises might be. So this is where things stand. I continue to strive for clarity and insight, and if I am successful, then I shall certainly share those field notes in the future.

Odds and Ends

To round out this issue of *Views from the Borderland*, I have a couple of other field notes to offer. These both relate to the overall theme of working with Gaia or developing a Gaian orientation to life which, as I indicated, seems to be becoming a major focus of my work as my own inner colleagues undergo a shuffling.

Intra-Gaian Collaboration

About a month ago, one of the new individuals who has become part of my "Pit Crew" said something provocative. He said, "I am not a subtle being. You are not a physical being. We are both Gaian beings." Having said this, he left to allow me to reflect on what he'd said.

It was clear that he was establishing a larger category of identity which would promote the cause of unity. It was as if a Greek were to say to me, "I'm not a Greek and you're not an American. We are both humans, citizens of the world." This doesn't change or invalidate the fact that we both have different national identities and belong to different cultures, but it emphasizes that we also have a larger, common identity, one that can draw us into a closer relationship. For that matter, it would be like saying that a whale and a human being are both mammals, even though both live in totally different environments. It's a statement of connectedness.

Though surprising, I took this contact and this statement to be another way of approaching the overall theme of "Gaian unity". As I've said, this seems to be the theme upon which my inner colleagues are now focusing.

A couple of days later this being returned and had this to say:

Pitt Crew Member: You must understand that when I and others like me think of ourselves as we exist in our world, we do not think of ourselves as "subtle beings". Nor do we think of our environment as a non-physical one. It is perfectly substantial to us. Likewise, we could easily think of you in your world as a subtle being, for when we approach you and seek to make contact, you are often insubstantial and misty to us. This is a consequence of existing in different frequencies of life and energy.

But this is something you already know, and it wasn't the central part of the point I wished to make. Many types of beings, not just those who, like me, have had human incarnation, are now engaged in building bridges with incarnate human consciousness and with the human world of activity in order to help during a time of transition. We seek to enlarge the conditions of wholeness which Gaia needs for its own well-being and evolution. We seek to promote a planetary perspective, one in which you see yourselves not simply as individuals or as human beings but as planetary beings, Gaian beings.

One of the stumbling blocks in this work is that you create categories that are too restrictive and narrow to convey the true nature of the world around you. You are very good at dividing the world up but not so good in seeing how it functions as a whole. The distinctions you create often blind you to what is really there. Thus, you distinguish between the organic and the inorganic but fail to see the life that suffuses both. You distinguish between plants and animals but fail to see the depth of intelligence within both. You distinguish between yourselves and the rest of nature, failing to see how connected and interdependent you are. It is not the distinctions that are at fault but how you apply and use them.

In this context of useful but limiting distinctions, I would have you consider the physical world and what you term the subtle worlds. You and I occupy different dimensions of life. This obviously cannot be ignored. But we are both part of the whole life of the same planet. I am in my world and you are in yours, but we are both part of Gaia. This is what I would like you to think about.

You are engaged in a project of cooperation and collaboration across dimensional boundaries. You think of it as a project of partnership between the physical and subtle worlds. I would like you to think of it instead as an activity taking place within the overall body and beingness of Gaia. Think of it as "Intra-Gaian Collaboration." To think in this way, we believe, will enhance both your sense of Gaia itself and your ability to engage and collaborate with us, for how you think can be either a bridge or a wall between us. Use this idea of our Gaian commonality rather than our dimensional differences as a focus for your reflection and thinking and see where it takes you. Blessings!

NOTE: *As the last of the preceding pages shows, I used* Views *as a way to highlight my own growing edge, the places where I was learning, and where nothing was certain and mistakes could be made. What I was sharing were my raw experiences with subtle phenomena and forces. It was as important to me to show where I was having difficulty or was wrong as it was to show my successes. I wanted to illustrate* process, *not simply deliver conclusions*

I believe this vulnerability was key to the success of the journal as it invited others to share their growing edges, too, and to be vulnerable in doing so. This led to some amazing conversations and insights in the Subscriber Forums. We were mutual explorers, sharing our field notes, our blind alleys as well as our breakthroughs.
—Sept. 2025

CHAPTER TWO
Issue 18, September, 2015

Understanding Gaia

As readers of this journal know, I've been feeling called to investigate as much as I can the nature of Gaia, the planetary spirit whose life and consciousness ensouls this world. This proved to be challenging, as I indicated in the last issue, because Gaia is not simply another subtle world being that one might contact. There's a difference, after all, between a fish in the ocean contacting another fish, even one that is significantly larger—like a minnow seeking contact with a whale—and that same fish contacting the ocean itself. It's not simply that the ocean is orders of magnitude larger than any fish; it's also that which enables the fish to live and move about as a fish.

I've heard and read of people speaking of attunement and alignment with Gaia as an enhanced form of environmental awareness, that the more in harmony we can be with the Soul of the planet, the more we can act with ecological wisdom and wholeness. I'm sure this is right, but for me, it's not the primary motivation for this investigation. Put simply, I feel that in understanding Gaia, we gain deeper insight into who *we* are. To discover Gaia is to discover ourselves…and much more besides. We are the fish discovering what kind of creature lives and swims in an ocean.

Mariel's Hint

Readers of the last *Views from the Borderland* may remember that I felt I was not able to go as far into my exploration into Gaia as I had wished. I had bits and pieces of experience and information, some of it gained by personal observation and some given by inner colleagues whose communications I shared in that issue. But I felt something was missing or that I was not putting the information I had together properly. The feeling was as if I'd been following a trail but had gone off-road or had missed a turning so that the trail had become lost.

If you're lost in the woods, sometimes the best action is to do nothing but sit and get your bearings. Especially if the "woods" are the subtle realms, wandering about only creates more confusion. The "forest" knows where you are, and if you wait, it will find you.

I have felt, as I said, that the need to understand Gaia isn't arising in me out of intellectual curiosity or a desire to have some esoteric knowledge; it's been a sense of calling tied to my work with Incarnational Spirituality. In my world view, our incarnations emerge out of and thus are part of and contributing to Gaia's incarnation. Understanding Gaia is important to fulfilling this participation. It seemed to me, then, that if this calling were genuine, help would find me and put me back on the trail I felt I'd lost.

So, after I finished the last issue, I took a break from this particular exploration, allowing it all to settle down within me. My only moves in a Gaian direction were to take time just sitting outside and appreciating the life around me. I wasn't trying to attune to anything in particular but just communed with the trees and plants, the birds and any other creatures that I could see and feel in my vicinity, as well as with the mountains that surround this area where I live. Rather than putting my focus and attention on Gaia, I simply allowed myself to sink, with love, into the world around me, without thoughts, without words, and without expectations.

As it happened, help did come from an unexpected but not altogether surprising source. I awoke one morning with a clear sense of Mariel's presence. Mariel is the Sidhe woman who was my primary contact and inspiration for the co-creation of the *Card Deck of the Sidhe* with my Lorian colleague, Jeremy Berg. She is also the main contributor to my book *Conversations with the Sidhe*. Weeks and months can go by without our being in contact, but she can show up when needed or when she has something to offer to whatever project I'm working on. In this instance, it was she rather than one of my usual inner colleagues who became my trail guide.

Mariel communicates with me primarily in two ways. The first is through a form of telepathy—or something equivalent—in which her thoughts and words are transmitted directly into my mind. This is usually the mode she uses when she comes close to my world—when she "drops in", so to speak. The second is a form of participatory communion in which my consciousness becomes part of her own, and I'm able to see and experience what she does as if I'm sharing her point of view. This second mode is the one that enables me to visit her world. I'm not really traveling out of my body but rather traveling within her energy body, so to speak, or within her mind.

Waking up and feeling Mariel's presence and invitation to accompany her, I was in an ideal state to respond, as I was in that liminal space between sleep and full wakefulness. So I accepted her invitation, and found myself in a place to which she has taken me several times before. We are standing at the edge of a meadow where it meets a forest. Off in the distance a large mountain rises, reminiscent to me of Mt. Rainier in my world. Next to us is a small building that I think of as a chapel. It has living quarters within it but it's primarily a temple, a place of inner work. It's where Mariel does her work as a star priestess (at least, that is what I call her) and where she can stay for extended periods, though apparently she has a home in a nearby Sidhe town in that particular parallel vibratory world that she inhabits.

Of course, all this may simply be how my mind interprets the information, the energies, and the fields that I perceive when in this communion with Mariel's consciousness. Over the past four years or so that Mariel and I have been in contact, this particular place has remained consistent whenever she's brought me here, so I assume that how it looks to me is relatively close to how she experiences it as well, but when dealing with worlds as fluid as those of the Sidhe, I never really know. What I do know is that the qualities and presences that I would identify with "forest", "meadow", "mountain", and "temple" in my world are the same as what I experience in Mariel's environment, though they are more vibrantly alive in her world than they are in mine.

In this instance, we go into the temple, which I experience not at all like entering into a building—I really have no idea what it looks like inside, although as I said, I have a clear impression of personalized living quarters off to one side, as if on the other side of a wall. When I'm outside, the building seems small to me, more like a cottage, but when she brings me inside into the temple area, it's always as if I enter into a place that seems without dimensions: vast, and alive with vibrancy and expectation. My guess is that when we enter her temple, her own consciousness undergoes an expansion which, because I am participating in it, gives me the feeling of stepping into spaciousness.

At this point, I am aware of my body lying in my bed and at the same time of being in this spacious and expectant silence within her temple. Almost no time has passed since Mariel had appeared, and aside from inviting me to go with her, she has said nothing. Now she turns to me, smiles and says, "Observe."

What happens next is hard to describe. The space we

were in suddenly took on definition and seemed to open up, as if it had become a funnel with Mariel and I at the wide end while the other end became a channel of Light. This extended into a realm that was filled with a sparkling, silvery Light that became brighter and more intense the further one went into it. It was like looking into a silvery sun, and I had the immediate impression that I was looking into the heart of a star. But it was not hot, as our sun would be, nor was it painful to look at in spite of its intensity. I felt enriched and energized just looking at it.

As I watched, the silvery Light poured down the channel into us, and I had a sense of an immensely powerful, loving, and caring Presence in the midst of a company of such Presences. I felt my mind flooding with information. Then the vision stopped as Mariel closed down the channel. I found us standing outside her temple again.

"That is sufficient for now," she said.

"Thank you. I felt like I was in the heart of a star," I said.

"You were," Mariel replied. "It was Gaia. Gaia is the incarnation of a star."

This came as a complete surprise, so much so I found myself fully back in my body, filled with a need to process this insight. The link with Mariel faded into the background, and I had to get up to think about what I'd just seen and experienced. I needed to jot down notes while it was fresh in my mind.

The Stellar Realm

Broadly speaking, there are two kinds of science: applied science, which looks for ways of directly benefiting human life, and "pure" or theoretical science, which explores why things are they way they are, whether that information can be put to practical use or not. In a way, my own inner researches are the same. For the most part, I engage with the subtle Borderlands and beyond in order to gain insights that will be helpful to individuals in their everyday lives; Incarnational Spirituality is an example of this kind of work. My explorations of the principles of manifestation or of energy hygiene are another. I'm not really interested in mystical, esoteric or occult information for its own sake. Still, I do have experiences of the subtle worlds or contacts with subtle beings that do not immediately suggest any useful application or insight—at least not that I'm able to see at the time. Sometimes, the odd or unexplainable experience turns out later to have significance and meaning I was unable to discern at the time it happened.

I've been aware most of my life of a higher frequency of life and consciousness that I call the "stellar realms" in much the same way that on a physical level, I'm aware of the stars. The night sky is beautiful, awesome, and inspiring, filling me with wonder, but on a practical level, the stars are many light-years away and beyond my reach. They do not affect my everyday waking life. The same could be said of the stellar realms. That they are important to the life and well-being of the Earth and of humanity is clear to me, but precisely how has not always been apparent. Though I've always felt drawn to and connected with these realms, they have remained overall abstract and mysterious to me.

Many years ago, my subtle world mentor John took me to a realm at the edge of the planetary aura or subtle field. I traveled in much the same way as I did with Mariel, "piggy-backing" on John's consciousness and energy field. To my human mind, the place where we went looked like a grassy field ending in a cliff which appeared to be the edge of the world. The land simply stopped, and beyond it was outer space, filled with stars. There was a faint film, like a thin force field, between the land and the cosmic realm beyond. As John and I stood there, I became aware of thin, narrow beings that looked like giant blades of green grass with eyes rising out of the land around us. These beings were beautiful and tall, easily seven or eight feet in height as my mind interpreted them, and very graceful for entities without arms or legs. As I watched, they would rise into the air, swooping forward and passing through the force field to disappear into the starry cosmos beyond. "These," John said at the time, "are the World Soul's emissaries to the stars."

As he said this, I was also aware of similar beings, made up of a shimmering silvery Light passing through from the other direction to disappear into the earth around us. Without being told, I knew that these were reciprocal beings entering the earth carrying energy from the stars.

This was a very vivid experience, and at the time, John's purpose in showing me this was to illustrate how our world is energetically connected to the larger cosmos. Of course, these connections take form, at least in my perception of them; the beings John showed me, which I dubbed "space elves," are only part of the many ways in which sacred energies circulate between our world and the rest of the universe. But John's point was that there were cosmic subtle realms as well as planetary ones.

For me, these larger domains of life and consciousness and the circulation of subtle energies that extended beyond the subtle energy field of the Earth became what I called the "stellar realms". For a long time, this was largely an umbrella term for me which meant simply subtle energies and frequencies "not originating from the Earth" but which did not do justice to the complexity and richness of the energy ecology represented by these realms. It's commonplace these days to say that we're all made of "star-stuff", since most of the atoms that comprise our bodies were created in the nuclear processes at the heart of stars. The same can be said of our inner nature. John and other subtle colleagues have always held that the original spiritual beings from whom the souls of humanity have, for the most part, developed came from the stars, that is to say, from higher dimensions of stellar or cosmic life. We are star-stuff in our souls as well as in our bodies. But we are also beings of Earth, children and partners of Gaia, and this is where our primary evolutionary focus has been—and still is, for that matter.

For this reason, for me the role of the stellar forces and of the stellar realms has not always been clear in the context of our everyday, planetary incarnations and lives. From time to time I would have experiences of subtle energies that seemed to originate from some stellar source, but aside from acknowledging them, I didn't know except in a few cases what their purpose was or how best to interact with them. In exercises I would create for my classes, I would feel impressed to ask people to attune to the stellar realms but it wasn't always clear what this meant. I simply proceeded in faith that in doing the exercise, a benefit would emerge from giving attention and attunement to these extra-planetary vibratory frequencies. In some ways, they served as a metaphor for me of those forces that help us to move beyond our boundaries so that we can "think outside the box" and see our world and our lives from a larger perspective.

On the whole, though, I considered that attuning to the stellar realms fell into the category of "theoretical research" since it was not always evident how any information or energies obtained by attuning to these frequencies could be applied. The cosmic realms were fascinating and conducive to wonder but it was in working with the planetary frequencies that practical benefits could be had.

This began to change while I was working with Mariel on the *Card Deck of the Sidhe* and subsequently on *Conversations with the Sidhe*. She was someone who actively and regularly worked with stellar energies of various kinds. In fact, Mariel has identified herself as a "star-priestess." For her, in her world, stellar energies are very practical. When she's drawing this star-energy down and radiating it out, everything seems to come more alive around her; it reminds me metaphorically of watching the drooping leaves of a plant that's been without water revive when the plant receives moisture.

In any event, my association with Mariel has enhanced my own attunement to the stellar realm so that from time to time, I'm able to form a closer connection with that level of being than I have in the past. It's been evident that stellar energies of various kinds are important to the life of Gaia in much the same way that sunlight is important to my life and that of all physical creatures here on Earth. I've been working to understand just how these energies are important in our physical incarnations. It's been part of my research into Gaia. But the experience with Mariel opened up a new level of understanding.

A Stellar Incarnation

The information that Gaia was the incarnation of a star was surprising enough. But I was more interested in the other information I'd received while in the temple with Mariel. Perhaps it had been a communication from Gaia, perhaps from Mariel. Perhaps it had even been a memory, an ancient recognition and remembrance from my own soul. Or it might have come from a different source altogether. I don't know, and it doesn't really matter. The point was that I had a whole new insight into the stellar realms that I had not had before.

I experienced these realms as filled with beings who

distilled from the Unmanifest, the Generative Mystery that is the Source of all that is in our universe, the primal quality of Life itself. This is the *holopoietic* animating force behind the cosmos and its evolution and unfoldment. It meant that the stellar realms—or at least that part of those realms to which Mariel and I were attuned in that moment—were really the realms of Life. This Life-Force is then disseminated in various ways. One way is into actual physical stars where the nuclear processes create most of the atoms necessary for physical life as we know it to exist. Another way is into the dimensions from which souls as particularized manifestations of life emerge. But for some within the stellar dimensions, a third way is to foster the development and evolution of life in a "hands-on" way, carrying the life force directly into physical matter and physical embodiment. This is the way that creates a "star-soul" that can in turn become a planetary spirit. It is the way of planetary incarnation, the path that our Planetary Spirit, Gaia, is following.

What does it mean for a star to take incarnation? I've always seen stars such as our sun as the physical embodiment of a stellar being. And many years ago, I was shown an image of the Earth as a "green star", a star of life radiating the spiritual energy of the biosphere into the cosmos. But I did not think of this as a manifestation of the stellar realms or of an actual stellar being. I've been thinking of a star somewhat metaphorically as a generative, radiant source. In such a context, then, indeed the Earth is a star, and as generative beings, we are "stars" as well. But this is different from a vast cosmic being whose native state is within the stellar realms taking on form as a planet in order to carry into physical expression the life force that it helped manifest in the first place. What Mariel had shown me was a wholly new idea.

A few days after having this experience, Mariel returned

and offered her own comments on the matter:

> MARIEL: The stellar realms are vast and many-layered. They lie close to the mystery of Divinity, and none at our level of consciousness may fully penetrate or know their nature. As physical stars are the wombs of matter, so the stars of spirit are wombs of life. They are the birthplace of angels and archangels, the matrix from which planetary spirits emerge.
>
> When I attune to these realms, I am attuning to a reservoir of love and caring from which Life flows, and I draw that Life into my realm for the benefit of my people and my world. You have understood my function as that of a priestess to the stars, and this is true as far as it goes, but I am more accurately a priestess of Life, the stellar Life that is the silvery blood of the cosmos, energizing all.
>
> I told you that Gaia is the incarnation of a star. It is more accurate to say that our Planetary Spirit is the incarnation of the stellar realms, for the stellar beings whose fields of consciousness make up those realms are not individuated in a way you would understand. But they are not a single consciousness either. They possess multiple fields of intent and awareness, and some of these are living currents of purpose that seek to reach down into the furthest depths of matter to create avenues for the expression of Life. Out of these currents arises a configuration of will and love that I might call a "star-soul". It is a particular focus of the collective intent of the stellar realms as a whole, and from this emerges a planetary spirit such as the one ensouling our world, the one we are calling Gaia, who is capable of working in the realms of both subtle and physical matter.
>
> In this, Gaia is not so different from you or me, for our own sacred identities arise from currents of intent within

the life and mind of the Sacred, and these identities in turn spawn the souls that generate our respective incarnations on many levels, including the one you occupy. The details differ, but the overall pattern is a universal one.

As I said in the last journal, my "Pit Crew"—the assemblage of subtle beings who work with me on a somewhat regular basis—has been changing. Colleagues who have been with me for several years have been moving on and new individuals have been taking their place. It reminds me of a shift change at the Boeing plant near where I live! The new arrivals have for the most part been less focused on individuals and more on the life and unfoldment of Gaia.

After thinking about Mariel's information for awhile, I decided to contact one of the "new guys" to see if he (or she) had any further insights into the matter. The being who responded presented itself to me as a radiant sphere, neither male nor female, and seemed to me part of an angelic or Devic line of evolution. Nevertheless, it seemed perfectly comfortable communicating in human terms with me and was fully conversant with the questions in my mind. Here is my interpretive translation of its communication:

> INNER CONTACT: Greetings and blessings. Your questions about the stellar realms need to be properly framed. There is the universe of stars that you see around you. It is a cosmic ecology that is rich and diverse, one that rightly fills you with wonder and a sense of the vastness of being. Within it are streams of life, energy, and consciousness that flow between the stars, and some of these engage your world in different ways. This is the realm of stars, the cosmic stellar realm which might more properly be thought of as the cosmos.

What Mariel showed you is something different. What you experienced was the realm of beings from whose activity stars emerge. They act to generate the fires of life that fill the cosmos. This stellar realm is not simply a collection of stars but the generative heart of the universe; it holds the mystery of generativity itself.

One way in which this generativity is manifested is through the energetic radiance of a star, both as a physical entity and as its inner Logos or Spirit. In this act, they help to structure and hold the architecture of the cosmos as you know it and fill it with life. But a stellar being can be radiant and generative in other ways. This is the case with Gaia. Just as your sun generates and radiates energy in the form of waves and particles of light, so Gaia is a stellar being that generates and radiates energy in the form of waves and particles of life. All the beings upon the earth are like rays of energy and Light. You are a "photon" of life, and humanity is collectively a wave of life.

The stellar being who incarnates as your sun is akin to the stellar being who incarnates as your Earth; both are part of the same domain of spirit. One is following a path of light, one is following a path of life. The end result is very different in the physical realm, but there is equivalency in the generative spirit behind each.

Are all planets incarnations of stellar beings? No. Are all planets with life incarnations of stellar beings? No. But Gaia is, and this is what gives your world such a rich, diversity of life-forms. But even this is not fully what distinguishes your Planetary Spirit as the embodiment of a stellar being. Here we touch on a mystery that is central to your human experience.

Gaia is a stellar being who is incarnating the qualities of the stellar realm into the physical realm for its blessing and transformation. In a sense, one of the highest of living frequencies is reaching down to become one with one of the lower frequencies of being. It is a great experiment, one involving more than just the human species but certainly one that affects your own destiny. In particular, it is nurturing the arising of forms of life and consciousness that can embody, hold, and express the generative qualities and capabilities of the stellar realms. It is an experiment in transmitting and implanting aspects of its own nature into life-forms in both the subtle and the physical realms, creating, as it were, organic stars.

There is a sacrifice involved in this act for the star-soul that has become Gaia. It has set aside aspects of its own life to enter into communion with the depths of the material realm. In a manner of speaking, it has buried itself alive. It finds liberation in each of its children who can ignite their own star-souls within themselves. This is why humanity came to Earth eons ago, to assist in this experiment and to unfold the stellar potentials in its own collective beingness. For when you blended with Gaia at the beginning of your evolutionary journey, you gained access to its star-soul and to the stellar realms beyond. In your incarnational partnership with this world, you have gained a portal into the heart of stars and thus into your own star-like potentials.

Remember that what I share with you is a narrative designed for your mind; it is a seed of mystery that, if thoughtfully planted and watered, will blossom with further insights. I leave this to you with my blessings.

Envisioning Gaia

I often find it helpful when dealing with new information from the subtle realms to try to encapsulate it in a drawing.

Doing this helps me sort things out and gain a perspective on what I've experienced or observed. Of course, I'm no great artist, so my drawings are simple, even at times simplistic.

In the last issue of *Views from the Borderland,* one of my inner contacts spoke of the difference between Gaia as the Planetary Spirit and the planetary angel who overlights all living organisms within the biosphere, a being often referred to in popular culture as "Mother Nature." Combining this information with what Mariel had to say and the insights of the new being in my Pit Crew, I came up with this diagram of the four dimensions of Gaia from Star-Soul to the physical world and their correspondences within our own inner makeup from our "I" or sacred Identity to our physical body and personality. Uniting both and available to both are the Stellar Realms.

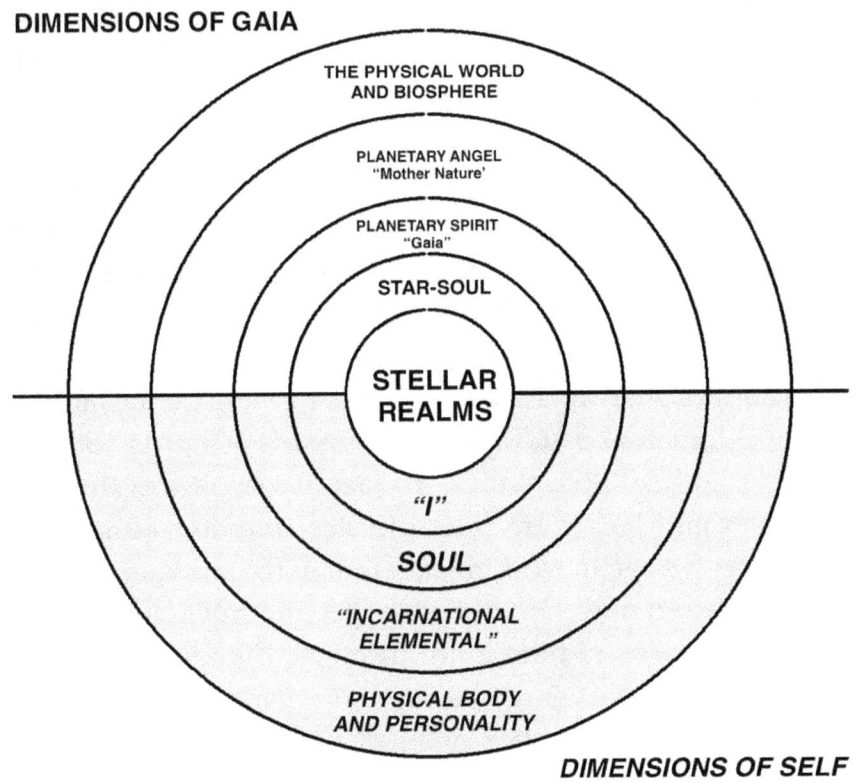

There are many ways to understand, interpret, imagine, and present the idea of Gaia. It can simply be the idea of a living planet. In James Lovelock's seminal book *Gaia: A New Look at Life on Earth*, he uses "Gaia" to refer to the self-regulating processes within the biosphere that give the planet characteristics similar to those of biological organisms; however, he stops short of seeing Gaia as a being with soul and spirit. On the other hand, many, if not most, ancient cultures did see the Earth as a god or goddess, or at least as a living entity possessing a spiritual as well as a physical reality. In my own world view, based on my perceptions and experiences, I see Gaia as an incarnating spirit, just as you or I or the maple tree in my backyard are incarnating spirits, though on a vastly different scale of life and consciousness.

However, the perspective offered by Mariel and by several of my newer "Pit Crew" colleagues, including the one whose communication I just shared, suggests that among other things, Gaia is a womb for seeding and nurturing living "stars", a strategy for developing beings and consciousnesses that can embody and express the generative powers of the stellar realms within the incarnate worlds of subtle and physical matter.

The idea that we are each a source that generates living energies much as a star generates light is a central concept in Incarnational Spirituality. In fact, it was one of the first lessons that "John", my non-physical mentor, taught me soon after we began working together in the summer of 1965, fifty years ago now. He did so by putting me in touch with a unique energy radiating not from my thinking or feeling or from my subtle energy nature but arising as a force from my life itself. I called this energy of life "Self-Light." It is unique to each person, a radiance of his or her sacredness, Sovereignty and individual beingness.

Incarnation is a form of spiritual work as the Soul engages with the subtle and physical dimensions of the incarnate realms. For some years, I understood Self-Light as a byproduct of this incarnational "work", much as heat is the byproduct of physical work. But the more I researched into the processes of incarnation, the more I understood that Self-Light wasn't a byproduct but rather was the direct expression of a fundamental generative ability. In describing this innate generative capacity in classes, I likened us to stars as a metaphor. What my new inner colleagues are suggesting is that this may be much more than a metaphor.

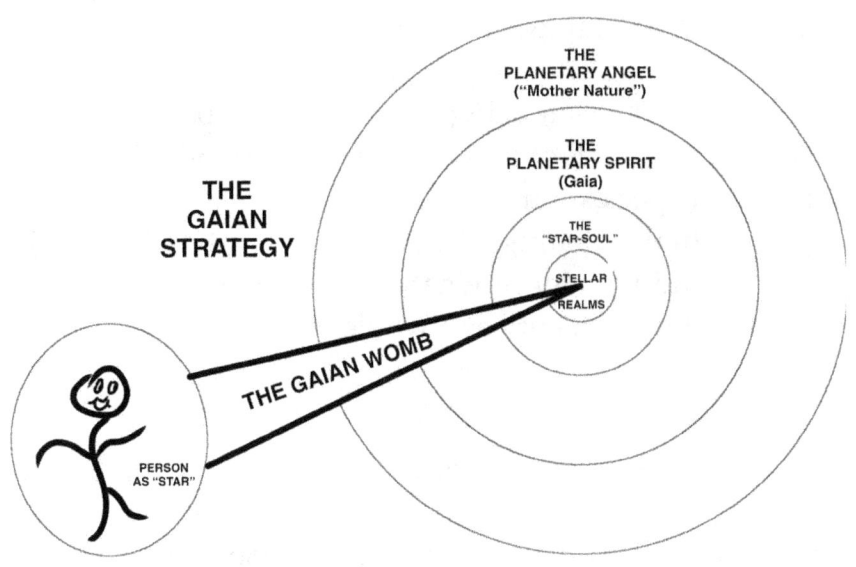

This illustration depicts for me a new way of envisioning Gaia, seeing it as a strategy—a womb—for unfolding in us (and undoubtedly in other species of physical and non-physical life as well) the capacity to manifest the generative spirit of the Stellar Realms: to bring forth the person-as-star. Gaia embodies not only the intent of a Planetary Spirit to provide an environment for the evolution of physical life but also the intent of a "Star-Soul" (and of the Stellar Realms as a collective field of consciousness and life) to foster in the depths of matter a conscious expression of the generative Light at the heart of stars.

These field notes would be incomplete without attempting to share the feeling tone of these experiences, that is to say, their impact upon me emotionally and energetically. When I was in Mariel's temple and felt the attunement with the star-heart of Gaia, I felt uplifted and valued. I felt a profound sense of caring and nurturing, not so much directed to me as a person but directed to the generative spirit within me. Actually, what it felt like was as if I were an egg and Gaia was a hen brooding over me to help me hatch—or more precisely, to help a generative consciousness and presence hatch in the form of a human being. I felt this both personally and collectively, that all of us—humans, Sidhe, and who knows what other species—are eggs in the process of development and eventual hatching. This felt very affirming of the splendor and wonder of what is incubating within each of us and within humanity as a whole.

A Gaian Yoga

The trajectory of my work over the past fifty years has been interesting. For the first five years when I was in my "apprentice" period (recounted in my book *Apprenticed to Spirit*), my focus was on the individual and the integration of soul with personality. It was an early attempt to formulate some of the principles that later evolved and matured into Incarnational Spirituality. Then in 1970, I went to Scotland and became the co-director of the Findhorn Foundation community. At that point, and for nearly twenty years after, I became a spokesperson for the idea of an emerging New Age. Nearly all my work focused on new cultural paradigms, societal change, and planetary transformation. Relating to Gaia as the living spirit of the biosphere was an important part of that work. In the early Nineties and for another twenty years, my work shifted again away from the planetary and back to a focus on the individual. This led to the development of Incarnational Spirituality.

But now I feel the wheel turning once more and another shift taking place back towards Gaia and the planetary whole, though this time it's not a moving away from the individual but towards the partnership, the synergy, of person and planet, individual and world. In the language of Incarnational Spirituality, the work is expanding to engage not only our own individual incarnations but the incarnation of Gaia as well.

With this in mind, the underlying question in my mind when making many of my contacts with subtle colleagues recently has been the nature of this relationship between ourselves and our world. Specifically, what practices emerge out of this partnership, if we conceive of the relationship as a partnership, as I do? What joins person and planet together spiritually and energetically? Put another way, what might constitute a "Gaian Yoga"?

Thinking about this in relationship to the information provided by Mariel and my inner colleague, I recast the earlier illustration on page 51 to show how we might relate to the different dimensions or definitions of Gaia. I show this next.

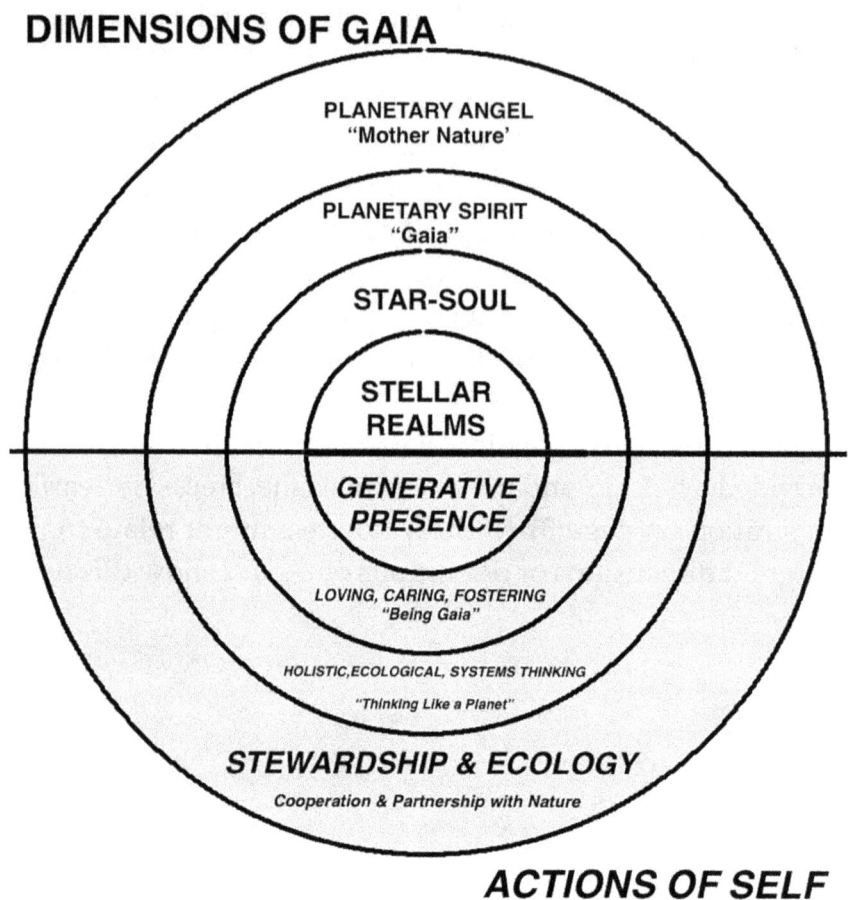

For example, if we are relating to what we customarily call Nature—the physical environment and biosphere—then our "yoga" might be all the ways we express stewardship, conservation, and ecological awareness. It's how we cooperate with Nature to create or maintain wholeness. In fact, "working with Gaia" is often understood and presented in just this way, with Gaia meaning the life and spirit of the natural world. Even though the overlighting spirit at this level may not be Gaia directly but rather one or more planetary angels, it's still within the overall life and energy field of the Planetary Spirit itself.

This level of "Gaian Yoga" is the easiest for people to understand and engage. We can all see the effects of environmental pollution and climate change, and while the necessary responses to restore wholeness to the system may be complex, they are well within the realm of physical action and perception. It does not take attunement to any subtle dimensions to clean up a polluted stream or to protect threatened species in order to preserve biodiversity.

The other three circles of engagement with the Planetary Spirit (Gaia proper), the Star-Soul, and the generative power and presence of the Stellar Realms are more subtle. Indeed, individually and, more importantly, collectively, these three levels or aspects constitute the arena (as well as the methodology) for subtle activism. It's easy to understand why they may not be understood or even accepted as having any reality. Cleaning up the air we breathe is a recognizable priority for health and well-being, but cleaning up the non-physical dimensions of the planet, such as the subtle energy environment that also surrounds and affects us, is not yet within the awareness of most people.

A "yoga" uniting us as persons with Gaia's different levels as I've been presenting them here would include (but not be limited to)

Learning to "think like a planet", i.e. to think holistically, ecologically, and with an awareness of whole systems, as a way of aligning with the perspective and work of Gaia as the Planetary Spirit; this is not simply intellectual or cognitive thinking—i.e., thinking *about* things—but what a mystic might call "heart thinking," thinking holopoetically with Presence and soul as well as with mind and emotions. The result of such thinking is not simply information or conceptual knowledge but connectedness, wholeness, and love.

Learning to *be* Gaia in oneself—a planet-in-miniature—as a way of aligning with the Star-Soul from which the Planetary Spirit emanates. The planet fosters life; "being Gaia" means discovering in ourselves the qualities and capacities that also foster, support, and empower life. This would involve learning to operate from a core of love, fostering, caring, compassion, joy, and other qualities that empower, uplift, connect, and create wholeness.

Learning to be a generative source of Life, a living star. This actually is a core objective in Incarnational Spirituality which views each person as a generative source. (Although I didn't have the information about the Star-Soul or the Stellar Realms I've presented here when I wrote it, my book *Journey into Fire* deals directly with attuning to and expressing our generative self.)

Engaging with Gaia—practicing a "Gaian Yoga"—would involve as many of these modes as we are able to embody. And as I hope you understand, the drawings I've offered here are only ways of highlighting these different modes and levels. The key fact is that Gaia functions in a seamless way in wholeness, its spirit permeating and pervading all five of the circles in Figure 1. It's not that the Star-Soul or the Stellar Realms are the "true" Gaia just because I've drawn them at the center. The "true" Gaia is what is constantly emerging and acting through the blending and interaction of all these "levels", and this includes what is happening in us as well. For we, too, in our inner nature and makeup as well as our physical bodies, are part of the "true" Gaia. A Gaian Yoga is a yoga of a person, standing in his or her Sovereignty, Self-Light, and Presence partnered with planet to affirm and express the generative wholeness uniting and living within them both. In effect, Incarnational Spirituality is a Gaian yoga.

Generativity

Exactly what does it mean to be "generative"? The dictionary defines *generative* as the capacity to create or to produce, and I have used the term to mean our ability to produce or create a wide range of subtle energies and thus to be a radiating source. To be generative, as I use the term, is contrasted with being a consumer, someone who simply receives and takes in material and energies from other sources. Of course, we do both in our lives.

In my inner work, I have come to distinguish two kinds of generative ability or generativity. We generate *content* in the form of thoughts, emotions, subtle energies, and spiritual qualities. We do this all the time; all beings do. But the kind of generativity represented by the Stellar Realms is the generation of Life and its capacities. This enhances the ability to be and to do. Life energy is directly nourishing and empowering to beingness, which I understand as the capacity to hold, to process, and to express content of one kind or another.

To use a kitchen metaphor, Life enhances and vitalizes me as a cook, which in turn enables me to work with the content of cooking, such as pots, pans, stoves, recipes, spices, vegetables, and so on.

When I speak of our being generative, it's this ability to radiate a primal force of Life that I have in mind. Stars do it. We can do it.

Here is what one of my subtle colleagues, a being I call Philip, had to say recently when I asked him his take on this topic:

> PHILIP: I understand your desire for precise definitions, for the ideas you work with and the subtle phenomena and conditions they represent can be slippery.

Our world doesn't have the same devotion to boundaries that yours does, so one thing can slide into another. Still, I would caution you about establishing categories that are too firm and definitions that are *too* precise. In translating from our world to yours, you want to leave room for things to breathe.

So it is in this case of being generative. I would suggest that you see *generativity* as you call it on a sliding scale. There is a spectrum of being generative, and each point along that spectrum has its value, though I grant you that some points are more fundamental and basic than others.

Let me see if I can illustrate what I mean. Imagine a village made of brick houses. If we begin with a child in this village, she lives in the houses, she plays with toys her parents provide her, she eats food that is prepared for her. She produces none of these things but in her joy and play and in her growing, she gives happiness to those around her. As she gets older, she learns skill in preparing meals for others. Now she is producing, though the food from which she makes her meals and the kitchen in which she creates them are provided by others.

As she grows older still, she learns how to build a home of her own with its own garden and kitchen. She also learns how to help others build or repair their houses. Now she is taking bricks, the basic building material of the village, and creating with them. She is productive at a new level.

Now imagine that she takes another step and learns how to make the bricks themselves that in turn are used to make the houses. For the village, this is a fundamental skill, for if there are no bricks, there are no houses, and if there are no houses, there are no kitchens, no places to make meals or to shelter children, no storage places for toys. To create the bricks that enable everything else to manifest is to be productive at a basic level. She is not simply generating playfulness and joy, not simply generating meals, not simply generating her own unique house. She is generating the wherewithal for the village itself to come into being. She is providing the means that allow others to be creative and build houses according to their own unique architectural visions.

There is no point in her life at which she is not generative, but there are many points in her life at which her capacity to generate expands and what she generates changes. She is always generative. Her generativity, however, changes in its effect upon others and in what it can do to empower others to be creative themselves.

The stellar realms, as my colleague has said and as Mariel has shown you, make bricks for the rest of the cosmic village. Gaia as a stellar angel knows how to make bricks, and humanity is here to learn this skill as well.

When you speak of being a generative self and of being a radiant source like a star, you are really talking about discovering and unfolding your innate skill at brick making. This is what it means to generate the energies of Life. You are a source of that which is used to build the cosmos, not at a physical level but at a spiritual, energetic level. You are able to provide bricks, energetically speaking. Being a brickmaker is part of the human heritage, part of who you are as an incarnate person who is also part of Gaia.

Even here there is a spectrum of possibility and effects. After all, you can make bricks of clay and mud but you can also make them of silver and gold.

Philip's comments are in keeping with the general thrust of information from my subtle colleagues. They are always affirming of our innate, incarnate human potential, while acknowledging that this potential is not always tapped or manifested in its fullness. Thus, with respect to the illustration on page 56, much of the modern world is still grappling with developing a sense of stewardship and ecological concern, much less expressing it in concrete actions (and in this respect, individuals are often far more advanced than their respective governments or collective institutions). We're having to relearn what so many of our ancestors took for granted: respect for "Mother Nature" and an understanding that we need to cooperate with her and not dominate her. When it comes to embodying and expressing a connection with the higher aspects of Gaia, including its Star-Soul and its generative nature, humanity as a whole has a way to go.

This is true with our innate condition of being generative sources. The first step is to accept that this is a reality within us—or at least a potential. It may then follow that the "bricks" we create—the life-enhancing force we generate and offer to the world as our Self-Light—are only made of clay compared to the gold of the bricks made by stellar beings themselves. But they're still bricks. Learning to make them is a major step to fulfilling the Gaian potential and promise within us.

Brickmaking

So how do we make "bricks"? It's a great metaphor, but how does it translate into practice. How do we express our "stellar," generative nature?

I don't think there's a specific practice or technique, though I'm always open to the possibility. "Brickmaking" in this metaphor is generating a life energy that fosters and empowers beingness itself. There are undoubtedly as many ways of doing this as there are beings who seek to do it.

I've been working with Self-Light for many years now and with the idea of Presence. I'm sure our generative abilities are related to both of these. But it seems in the context presented by Mariel, Philip, and my nameless contact, there is more to it as well, another layer to be uncovered.

I thought that since Mariel had introduced me to the idea of Gaia being an incarnate star and seemed to work with this level of stellar influence herself, it would be helpful to contact her again and ask her how she does it. Here is the response I had:

> MARIEL: Thank you for your question. I see that I have initiated a process of inquiry. This was not my intent; I was seeking to show you just what it meant to me to be a "star-priestess" and what "working with the stellar realms" entailed. I felt this would give you a deeper understanding of the Sidhe. But I'm glad it has stimulated further exploration on your part.
>
> I may not be as helpful here, though, as you may hope, since we are differently constituted. Our bodies are not constructed in the same ways, and the realm in which I live has fewer restrictions than your own. I am closer to the energetic aspects of my nature and of life itself than you are in your physical body. This means I can reach and blend with subtle forces in easier ways than you.
>
> However, I think there is a principle here that will work for you as much as it works for me. In order for me to channel the stellar energies of life into my world, I must find their equivalent within me. In other words, I hold these energies by becoming them. I am not simply a tube through which these energies pass. Indeed, that is not necessary, for stellar energies pass into my world—and yours—all the time without need of mediation. What *is*

needed are translation and integration, or, to use a different metaphor, digestion and assimilation.

In fact, even this doesn't describe the whole picture, for truly my world—and yours—are as much part of the Stellar Realms as those higher frequency dimensions to which you may give that name. I touch the substance of those realms when I touch the substance of my world. Do you see? It is like notes on a musical scale. All the notes are part of music, part of sound. When I do my work in my temple, I simply bring the octaves together so different notes come into a harmony within the greater melody of life. But I have to appreciate and sound my note to do so.

So when I enter my temple and prepare to reach into the stellar heart of Gaia and thence into the stellar realms, I focus myself in my body. Before I can find the star within the earth and its note, I must find the star within myself and its note. You already understand this principle as it is one of resonance. I find that which is life-giving in me and this puts me in touch with what is life-giving in the spirit of the Earth. I sing a note within me and the world star responds with its note to me, within me, around me, and through me.

In fact, the image of flow, though correct in one way, is misleading in another for it suggests something traversing a distance, something traveling from where it is to where it is not. It is more as if different voices, singing individually, are brought into harmony so that they sing as a choir, not necessarily as one voice but as a collaboration of voices in a seamless song. In such a moment, the singers are not hearing the music as if from afar. They are in the midst of the music. They are the music.

As I said, my physical constitution makes this relatively easy for me to do. I am more physically attuned to the flow and presence of energy than you are in your physical state.

But the principle should work for you in ways appropriate to you and your realm. Discover and focus on what is life-giving within you and see how you proceed.

The process that Mariel describes here is, in fact, a familiar one to me. It is summed up in the Hermetic axiom, "As Above, So Below" and its corollary, "As Below, So Above." When resonance is created, elements that are fractals or octaves of each other connect, and a flow—or a harmonization—results. To use Philip›s more mundane metaphor, we become brick makers by becoming the bricks.

I also realized communicating with Mariel that what she was describing had things in common with the practice of Grail Space. In fact, for some months now, I have been exploring the use of Grail Space to invoke, if that's the right word, or heighten the presence of Gaia within a particular space or area. In fact, in the last issue of this Journal, I described a particular experiment I've been doing which consists of "being a planet" in miniature, that is to say, attempting to generate a "Gaian field of energy" around myself. This experiment came out of a communication with Philip that in essence said much the same as Mariel said in the contact I just quoted.

At that time, I was attempting to contact Gaia by building a link of resonance. If I could find and hold in myself life-affirming qualities of love, nurturing, caring, fostering, and the like—the kind of qualities I feel Gaia expresses in holding all of us—then I felt I could forge a link to the Planetary Spirit. But as you know from that earlier issue, the experiment was not as successful as I'd hoped.

With the information that I've shared in this issue, all of which has come in the past three months, I look back on that attempt and realize that my error, as I said at the beginning of this issue, lay in trying to contact Gaia in the same way I might contact another subtle being. If we think of Gaia as an incubator, though, then what we want to contact is not the incubator itself but what is being incubated. Gaia *is* what is being incubated within us. To contact Gaia, we want to contact the spirit of Gaia gestating and unfolding within ourselves.

A "Deva" Of Artifacts

It's been a curious aspect of my inner development that from early childhood, I have been sensitive to the life within things. This has been especially true in recent years. My awareness of subtle lifeforms within objects, walls, rugs, floors, lamps, chairs, sofas, and so on—what might be called the "artifact spirits" or "artifact elementals" has been keener than a comparable awareness of the nature spirits that are part of the natural world. Years before I was able to perceive and contact the spirit of the maple tree in my back yard, I could perceive and contact the spirit of our house or the life within a piece of furniture. Those of you who have followed my writings over the years will know that I've discussed the life within things many times. In a way, I feel like I've been a spokesperson on behalf of the life and spirit within our artifacts.

The realm of our artifacts—all the built things that surround us every day and that we use in our lives—has been brought into existence by humans; in a way, it's a separate ecology from that of the natural world, though obviously interlinked. We have created new pathways for the evolution of consciousness within the forms and materials that we have shaped. In this realm, we are the formative forces; we are the "Devas". The question is, how good a job are we doing as Devas of Artifacts?

To the extent that we see our artifacts as pieces of "dead matter," the answer is not a very good job at all. We don't acknowledge the evolving life energy within our things and thus do very little to vitalize and energize that life through our blessings and the sharing of our own life energy. We may love the appearance and usefulness of our things, but this love is often superficial. We think of an artifact as an "it," not as a "thou," to use Martin Buber's wonderful distinction.

(The Grail Space exercise in Incarnational Spirituality is one way of remedying this as it's an experiment in establishing a collaborative and mutually empowering relationship with the things around us, seeing them as our energetic partners.

NOTE: *For those unfamiliar with the Grail Space, I include it in an appendix at the end of this book.)*

What does it mean to speak of the evolution of life within our artifacts? For instance, how is the living energy within my coffee cup evolving? It's not going to change its form or its function. It's not going to become a larger cup or a differently shaped cup. It's not going to evolve into a coffee pot or a cauldron.

In speaking about evolution or development within the realm of our artifacts, I am talking about the energy structure of the artifact. On the physical level, my coffee cup is made of a glazed ceramic which most likely is derived from clay. Its substance comes from the mineral world, from the body of the earth. For that matter, so does its energy structure, but this structure has now been influenced and molded by human imagination, creativity and use. As part of the human world, this living energy is now exposed to stimuli very different from what it would have known had it remained part of the soil. It is exposed to mental, emotional, and possibly spiritual forces it likely would not have encountered as simple clay and mineral substances; on the other hand, it is cut off from the nurturing energies of the earth itself. In the Gaian realm, it is seen by the nature spirits as something alive. In the human world, it is most likely seen as something "dead" and "inorganic". As clay, it is loved and held by the spirit of the earth; as a coffee cup, it is simply used, its living energy ignored or denied.

One of the differences between our world and that of the Sidhe is that in the latter, things are loved and appreciated not just for what they are as artifacts but for the underlying life force within them, which is seen as a sacred energy. I believe the time will come when we view the things of our world in this way, too; indeed, to me this is what Gaian consciousness is all about. At such a time, we as humans will truly take responsibility for the well-being and evolution of the living energy that temporarily is manifesting as one of our artifacts. But until that time comes, there's nothing stopping any of us from doing so individually. One way to practice a Gaian yoga is to consciously take on the mantle of being a human "Deva" of the artifacts around us.

Exploring A Practice

What might this look like? One way I have approached this in the past is through the practice of Grail Space. But since having the conversations with Mariel, Philip, and others that I've shared in this journal, I've been exploring other kinds of practices as well. Basically, I've been asking myself the question, "Given that as a human being, I share responsibility for the built world I inhabit (the world inside a house, apartment, office, factory, store, and so on), how can I be to this built world what Gaia is to the natural world? How can I be a Gaia to the artifacts around me?" This has led me to experiment with a practice of "being a planet."

For me, all work with the subtle dimensions begins with grounding myself in my physical body. I do not try to "center" myself as such as much as I hold in my mind the entirety of my body from head to feet and feel into its wholeness and coherency. I then do the same thing with my sense of personal identity, feeling and honoring my uniqueness as a person and attuning to the value and sacredness of my personhood; I call this "standing in sovereignty". It's important to me that I start any engagement with non-physical reality with a clear attunement to my physical nature and to my individuality. (I believe there is a sacred reason and purpose why we are physical beings who experience unique identities; I don't want to "transcend" my individuality; I want to honor it as a foundation from which a sacred space or *temenos* can emerge. This is Incarnational Spirituality 101!)

At this point, I take note of and connect myself in an honoring and appreciative way with my immediate physical environment. I realize that in this moment, I am part of a specific location filled with specific things, and as much as possible, I want to establish a loving relationship with where I am and with what is around me. This helps to create a solid "field" or aura of physically-grounded energy.

In effect, what I am doing is establishing myself in my thinking, my feeling, and in my physical sensations as a fractal of the planet itself. I am a physical entity surrounded by a non-physical field of energy; Earth is a physical entity surrounded by a non-physical field of energy. We operate on a vastly different scale, but the principle of life within us is the same.

When I ground my awareness in my body, stand in my sovereignty, and connect myself to my environment, I feel like I'm creating around me a tiny field of "planet-ness" or

"Gaia-ness" in which I seek to replicate as much as I can the love, the live-giving, and the blessing that the Earth holds for all beings whose lives it nurtures.

CHAPTER THREE
Issue 25, September, 2017

The Consistent Theme

Through all the years of my interaction and work with subtle allies and with the subtle worlds, there has been one consistent theme. Sometimes it has been in the foreground and sometimes in the background, but it's always been there like the base notes that hold the beat and rhythm on which a song's melody and arrangements ride. This theme is that significant changes are occurring in the life, the structure, and the energy of the planet. In the words of one of my subtle colleagues, "Gaia is going through the equivalent of an initiation, and everything is being affected."

Because the focus of this change and its primary effects are found in realms where time, as we measure it, has no meaning, I cannot say when this began. But the effects began rippling into the world we know, slowly at first, around the Sixteenth and Seventeenth centuries—though an argument could be made that they really began a couple of millennia ago with the incarnation of Christ. But that's something I'll explore with you in the next issue of *Views*.

Whenever these effects started, the time we live in, the Twentieth and Twenty-First centuries, has seen the ripples turn into a wave as profound changes are occurring in both the physical and subtle environments of the Earth. These changes are civilizational: the rise and fall of nations, the tensions between globalization and nationalization, liberalization and fundamentalism, conflicts between religions and cultures, accelerating technological change, global communication and social media networking shrinking the human world in which we live—and ecological: climate change, species extinctions, and so forth. The incarnate world is struggling with change. Part of this, at least, is due to transformations within the life of Gaia.

This fact of planetary change has been the context for all my work, indeed, for my life. My very first public lecture in 1964, when at age 19, I was asked to be the keynote speaker at a conference on the New Age, was regarding what my subtle colleagues said at the time about this transformation; it was this talk that launched my career and led to my leaving college to become a speaker and teacher on spiritual themes. The things I've done since then—my classes and lectures around the United States in the Sixties, my time at Findhorn as a co-director of that community, the founding of Lorian, my involvement with the New Age movement, my work with Incarnational Spirituality, the Sidhe, and now the exploration of Gaia, Gaianeering, and the emergence of *Homo Gaian*—have all been branches off the trunk of planetary transformation. In one way or another, each of these activities has been inspired or shaped by the need both to understand and to serve the changes that are in process.

The Initiation of Gaia

My contacts in the subtle worlds have been saying since 1964 that our planet is undergoing an initiation. They have been clear that this is not an event but a process, one that is unfolding in stages. Don't expect, they have said, any single, big event: no revelation or catastrophe that will change all things in one fell swoop. On the other hand, when I attune to this process of change, at times I feel as if it's something that's already happened and all that's left is the working out of the consequences. The difference in these perceptions, I'm sure, is because of differences in the scale of time between Gaia's experience and my own. An event happening immediately and completely in the higher wavelengths of the subtle worlds may take a thousand years or more to unfold and manifest in human time.

(**NOTE:** *There is also a difference in perception. Events in our world are usually defined by time and duration, but I have experienced that events in the spiritual worlds are more "spatial" in character. The image I have is of a complex mold being pressed into a receptive substance like clay, creating a picture. The picture on the mold is a whole, complete phenomenon, but the substance in which it is imprinting itself has temporality, that is, it is a substance involving time and duration. Thus, one element in the picture may be separated from another element by a temporal quality — let's say five years. From the picture's standpoint as a mold, it is whole and immediate — all the component elements are visibly present — but from the standpoint of the receptive substance with its temporal quality, there may be five years between the perception of one element of the picture and the perception of another. Time passes (or seems to pass) between on part of the impression and another, connected part.*

I have always experienced the New Age not as a series of events in time, in which the question "How long will it take" makes sense, but as a whole "picture" impressing itself into the energy and consciousness of the world and of humanity. It is here now in its entirety as a presence or as a "field" of beingness, even though it appears on the surface as if it takes years to manifest.

The paradox — so challenging to our engrained way of perceiving and thinking — is that we are in the New Age, the new world, both in the Now and in the Now and Then.)

The idea of "initiation" has different meanings. It can mean admittance into a group or organization; it can mean the beginning of something; it can signify a rite of passage, such as a child being initiated into adulthood. It almost always means a change from one state of being to another. What does it mean for Gaia?

My thinking about this now is different from what it was when I was in my early twenties and this idea of a "planetary initiation" was first broached by my subtle colleagues. In those days, I thought of initiation within an evolutionary context. It marked the completion of one stage of consciousness development and the entry into a more advanced stage. The true initiation was always an inner process, though it could be confirmed and assisted outwardly through some form of ritual and energy exchange celebrated by an initiator. It was a sign of progression.

As I've become older and more experienced with the nature of spiritual energy processes in the subtle worlds, I no longer think of initiation as being so structured. For me, initiation has ceased to be adequately described as a path with discrete stages. It's more organic than that and not so linear.

Part of the challenge is that initiation, in a spiritual or esoteric context, is often perceived as an evolution or development of consciousness. This is true up to a point, but the problem is with our understanding and definition of "consciousness." We think of this as a mental attribute, a synonym for awareness. On the higher wavelengths of life and beingness, though, consciousness is akin to a substance. It is the primal "matter" of creation.

This does not mean that "mind" is the supreme quality of the universe from which all things proceed, as was taught by the New Thought movements of the Nineteenth Century in America. The phenomenon of consciousness, however, is not the same as mind. It encompasses much more than what we understand and experience as "thinking."

If we are going to define initiation as a development of

consciousness, then we need to think of consciousness in a more holistic way, as encompassing the whole being. Really, it is the substance of which the being is composed, whether that being is an angel, a deva, a human, a tree, or a planet.

There are a growing number of scientists who are proposing what the ancient mystery teachings have held for millennia: that the fundamental nature of the cosmos is consciousness and that matter proceeds from consciousness rather than the other way around. What is not fully understood, I believe, by those claiming this, is precisely that consciousness when used in this context is not the same as mind or thought. Rather mind and thought, as we experience them, are specific manifestations of the substance of consciousness, particularly within the subtle and physical realms associated with incarnation.

I try to get around this confusion by substituting words like "Presence" and "being" for "consciousness" and using the latter in its more familiar meaning as a state of mental awareness and processing. But even these words are problematic. Such is the challenge of trying to render multi-dimensional, holistic realities in three-dimensional, linear language.

I bring this up because when we talk about initiations, we almost always refer to an initiation of consciousness in the sense of mind. But there can be initiations of the emotions and initiations of the body as well, as we know. It's not that we're insensible to such things, just that there are habits of thinking left over from the Age of Enlightenment in Europe in which thought and reason were privileged as the highest aspects of human development, far superior to emotions or to the body.

If we think about it, we know that in our own development—in our own "initiations," so to speak—

sometimes our bodies advance before our emotions or minds do (as in puberty), sometimes it's our feeling nature that takes the lead, and sometimes it's our thinking. It isn't always thinking or awareness—"consciousness"—that is at the growing edge. However, the true meaning of initiation isn't a matter of which part of us takes the lead and reaches a new stage of development but rather how we integrate the resulting changes. The purpose of initiation is holopoietic: the creation of wholeness.

If I understand this, then when I think about the "initiation" of Gaia, I realize that it doesn't matter what may have set it into motion or what changes are occurring. The important thing is the need to establish wholeness. Which, I believe, is the crux of the challenge facing humanity today.

It also casts a more comprehensive light on what my subtle colleagues have been saying all these years. In my twenties, I understood them as saying that the World Soul—Gaia—was going through changes to which we needed to adapt. We needed to change as well. But now I realize that while, yes, changes are occurring, the deeper process at work is one of maintaining and reestablishing wholeness.

It is really a process of deepening our understanding, embodiment of, and expression of the holopoietic impulse and spirit at the heart of Gaia, the stellar realms, and of the Sacred. A person could certainly have good reasons from calling this the Christ spirit at the heart of creation.

The Field of "New Gaia"

With this insight, I recently went to my subtle colleagues—my "Pit Crew"—and asked if they had anything to say about planetary changes, the "initiation" of Gaia, and humanity's current role. I had the following communication.

Subtle Colleague (SC): Initiation for us means a change that is systemic, not merely incremental. It affects the whole being, not a part of it. This change is not simply developmental. It is transformative. A threshold is crossed, and the being now organizes itself differently. A new way of life has emerged.

What precipitates this is an accumulation of energy, information, and connections causing changes which the being cannot integrate anymore within its current organizational structure to maintain its wholeness and coherency. It must re-organize itself. A new synthesis must emerge. The result is transformation.

Consider Gaia, the Identity and Presence ensouling the evolution of the Earth. It is receiving energy and information from many sources which it incorporates into itself, often creating change within the planetary system. Humanity itself is a source of such energy and change. Taken together, these changes are requiring a reorganization of Gaia's subtle energy structure. This is to synthesize a new state of integration and wholeness and to open the door to new possibilities.

Let us take a page from your own writing. In manifestation, you speak of a "New You." We could say that to accomplish this synthesis, a "New Gaia" has come into being. You may picture this as an expanding sphere of intention and energy, a field that embodies and transmits what is necessary to bring planetary life into an energetic state compatible with the new level of integration and wholeness. It is both the product of change and the initiator of change.

When we have spoken of the planet undergoing an initiation, it is this field and its effects as it pervades the incarnate realms to which we were referring. Evolutionary changes have reached a point where a new manifestation—you might even say a new incarnation—of Gaia's life has become necessary. This is altering the subtle body of the Earth, which you experience as the subtle realms and the subtle environment. This in turn is necessitating changes in the human subtle body. Those who have sensed this speak of an emerging new consciousness within humanity, but it is more than a simple change of awareness or worldview. It is a structural change in the way subtle energies are received and processed within and around you.

(**NOTE:** *These days, with more experience and insights under my belt, I would expand this understanding of initiation. It's more than just a change into something new; it's a re-embodiment of the originating impulse which can now take advantage of newer or different capacities. Thus, puberty doesn't change the individual into something or someone else. Rather, it expands the capacity of his or her fundamental humanness and individuality.*

In a way, initiation is a return to the source, the well-spring, of the incarnation, an amplification and renewed expression of the spirit or soul that gave birth to that initiation in the first place.

Thus, the initiation of Gaia is to become more stellar, more star-like, more of the originating spirit of Gaia, This of necessity draws humanity back to the originating spirit of its association with Gaia and the desire to more fully embody the holopoietic impulse that is at the core of it all. Our "initiation" then is a step backward into our past as well as a step forward into our future, but really, neither of these truly describes what is happening. It is a deepening into the Gaian Human that is always part of our present, however dimly or fully we manifest it. —Sept 2025).

I asked my subtle colleague if the changes brought about by the expanding field of the "New Gaia" were responsible for the challenges we were facing, such as climate change. Here is the response:

> SC: First, let me say that while from our level of life, we see this field as a solid wave, it does not manifest in that way on your level. This is entirely due to the way subtle phenomena manifest in the realm of time and space as you experience them. Thus, it may seem to you that the wave manifests as a series of changes spread over time, some linked in a visible causal manner and others seemingly unrelated.
>
> Further, this expanding field moves outward from the core of Gaia in ways that accommodate and are appropriate to the lives and structures which it encounters. It is not inherently destructive as the blast wave of a bomb would be. It is a wave of love and nurturing. However, its pressure to change and to renew can cause entrenched incarnate patterns, whether of matter or of consciousness and energy, to shatter and be destroyed. This is because they are not flexible enough to respond in a resilient and adaptive manner to this field.
>
> It may seem to you that all the disruptions and changes going on in your world must be due to this wave of transformation, but this is not so. The world is a complex system, even at your level. There are many influences at work, and many effects that you see have more than one contributing cause. You mention climate change. This is not directly an effect of the new Gaian field as it works through the incarnate world. Incarnate humanity is causing this or at least accelerating it. You are doing so not only through outer activity but through disruption of subtle patterns and flows. The mental and emotional projections of humanity are a causative factor here.

However, here is where it becomes complex to assign causation, for the expanding Gaian field is impacting the subtle bodies of humanity. Where old patterns and habits of thought and feeling resist change, disruption occurs which can in turn affect the natural phenomena. All things are interconnected. You cannot affect one part of the system without affecting the whole system.

Humanity has erected structures grounded in the past. Now that past is changing as a new future unfolds. What was solid turns into sand under your feet.

The way forward is through love. This is hardly a new message, but it really is that simple. Love yourselves. Love each other. Love the world. Be open to the sacredness within all things which is a radiance of love. But we fear the resistance to love will make the encounter with the New Gaia more challenging and impactful than it needs to be. This is where humanity needs help, to learn the art of creating wholeness which at bottom is the art of creating love.

(**NOTE:** *Again, I would add here that the civilizational structures we have created are, in many respects, unable to serve us now because they are locked into temporality, into time. It is not whether they are old and or the past or novel and of the future. It's that they are not attuned to the present or to the holopoietic heart-energies that operate in the Now. Love makes us attentive to — and orients our intention towards — what is present rather than to what has been or what might be. — Sept. 2025)*

"You are Gaia."

It is often the case when I have an engagement with a subtle ally that others may show up later, or sometimes immediately, to comment on what the first ally had to say or, more likely, on how I am understanding what he or she had to say. This happened in this instance.

I should say by way of explanation that the group of subtle allies whom I call my "Pit Crew" all share a field of energy defined by a common purpose. They are linked together, but they do not all occupy the same wavelength of energy and consciousness and thus they do not all share the same perspective. Some are much closer to the incarnate world that I occupy and others are farther away. Most are somewhere in-between. If I were to draw the common energy field embracing my Pit Crew, it would look something like an egg with one or two individuals at the "bottom", one or two at the top, and most clustered somewhere in the middle.

The message I shared above came from an individual comfortably in the middle. The commentary that came afterward came from a feminine presence who is at the very top. This, as I said, gives her a different perspective on things. For convenience, I often call her "Mary." Here is what she had to say:

> MARY: I was aware of your question when you framed it. After all, you directed it to any of us who cared to answer! I felt that my colleague who responded said what needed to be said. However, as my colleague was speaking with you, I could not help but observe the images forming in your mind. They arise inadvertently from habit, I know, from a way of thinking common to incarnates. Still they give an inaccurate picture. It's important to recognize that the field of which my comrade spoke is not coming *from* Gaia and then affecting life in our world. It is happening *within* Gaia. Remember, we are all Gaia. You are Gaia. All who read your words are Gaia. The field, the wave, however you think of it, is not coming from the outside.

It is not something Gaia is doing *to* us, do you see? It is a process in which we are participating and to which we are contributing in our own ways.

Yes, it is a force to which you must respond, but it's a force arising from within you, from within all of us, whether on my level of life or on yours. We are part of the system that is changing and adapting. Our response must be both inward to what is arising and outward to what is occurring. We unfold in both directions as Gaia transforms.

If you understand this, you will not think of yourselves as victims but as participants and co-creators. You will feel life's reaching for new horizons, new capacities, new connections, and you will feel this within you.

Just remember. You are the Gaia that is changing.

Blessings!

There are undoubtedly many responses we can make to the changes in the world and in us. One response is through what my Lorian colleague Jeremy Berg calls "Gaianeering."

Gaianeering

Gaianeering is the art of creating wholeness with and within the field of a "New Gaia." To see what this can entail, we need to look at the ways in which we may interact with this expanding field. Although there are many such options, I choose to emphasize four of them as representative, each of which can be represented by a way of understanding Gaia and by a key word. I think of them as the "four Faces of Gaia." These are:

- Gaia as self-regulating biosphere; the keyword is **PARTICIPATION**.

- Gaia as a way of seeing and understanding the world; the keyword is **PERCEPTION**.
- Gaia as a subtle Presence, the World Soul, plus the collective spirit and energy of all the lives that participate with it to form the Earth; the keyword is **PARTNERSHIP**.
- Gaia as a new consciousness within individuals; the keyword is **PRESENCE**.

Gaianeering is the art of bringing these four perceptions or aspects of Gaia into expression as a living wholeness within us and within our world. Let's look at these four more closely.

Participation (Gaia As Biosphere)

This is Gaia as proposed and explained in the Gaia Theory, initially proposed as a hypothesis by James Lovelock and later elaborated in collaboration with microbiologist Dr. Lyn Margulis. Here, Gaia is a codeword for the synergistic relationships and interconnections between the organic and inorganic parts of the planet. These relationships, developed over millennia, create systems and feedback loops that regulate weather, temperature, and other environmental factors to create conditions favorable to life. These self-regulating systems and their interconnections suggest the biosphere is acting as a single organism, a living planetary being: Gaia, in Lovelock's term.

I knew both Lovelock and Margulis. In conversations with them, it was apparent that Dr. Margulis doubted Gaia was a true organism; she saw it more as an emergent "system of systems" acting in complex ways to maintain an environment that would sustain life. In a way, Gaia was a homeostatic loop of life sustaining life. If "Gaia" possessed any consciousness at all, she said to me once, it would be something equivalent to that of a single-celled organism.

Lovelock, however, championed the idea that Gaia was indeed a planetary being, a true organism, though he agreed with Margulis that if it did possess consciousness of some nature—and my impression was that he felt that it did—it would be at a rudimentary level.

What both scientists agreed on was the sensitivity of Gaia's internal systems—the interrelationships between organisms, weather, temperature, and so on. Both agreed that human activity was coming dangerously close to disrupting some of these systems or causing them to fluctuate towards extreme and unstable behavior. Climate change and global warming were indications of this, though there were others. In their view, it was possible to "kill" Gaia by so altering environmental conditions that the homeostatic stability—the capacity of Gaia to self-regulate in favor of life—could be lost, with catastrophic results.

For Lovelock and Margulis, the importance of the Gaia Theory was not that earth was itself a living organism but that whatever it was, its balanced systems could be upset by human activity. Gaia, for them, was a call to change how we interacted with the earth and to realize that we could not continue to act as if the planet were somehow separate from us. We were an integral part of the web of Gaian life, and if that web were destroyed, we would be lost with it. In other words, whether Gaia is a planetary organism or not, we need to participate in its life as if it were.

The act of Gaianeering in this instance, then, is to help maintain and nurture the many environmental systems that sustain the balance of life on earth. It is to act in a "Green" and ecological manner.

This is the most familiar form of Gaianeering: participation in the wellbeing of the biosphere. It consists of all actions we take to preserve, defend, and nurture Nature and its interconnected, interdependent ecosystems. The question a Gaianeer would ask is, "What can I do in the context of my life to help my world." Whatever we do to "green" our lives is an act of Gaianeering on the physical level.

As so much is already written and available on strategies and actions about this, particularly with the onset of climate change, I don't feel I need to say much about it here. We can research those personal actions and choices we can make in our own lives and circumstances, such as how to utilize and conserve energy, the kind of products and goods to use that support the earth, and so on. There are a great many resources available online, in magazines, and in books to aid us with this.

We can also help support those people and organizations that are actively working on behalf of nature and the world's ecosystems, trying to minimize, change or prevent the negative impacts of human activity. For instance, one of the speakers at the recent Lorian Gaianeering Conference was Vance Martin, the executive director of the WILD Foundation. This is a non-profit environmental organization whose vision is "to inspire a world that protects at least half of all nature on Earth in a connected way for the benefit of wilderness and communities." Allied with the Lorian Association, it is one of hundreds of such organizations around the world seeking to protect and serve nature and the environment.

There are political and economic choices we can make. We can vote for those leaders and representatives who will support and implement policies that benefit the ecosystems of the world (which, remember, include us). We can use our financial resources, either through our purchases or our investments, to empower those companies and businesses who are demonstrating their care for the earth and for environmental wholeness.

In other words, we can make decisions and take actions to be physical, environmental, political, economic, and social Gaianeers in whatever ways are appropriate in our lives.

Perception (Gaia as a Way Of Knowing)

Second, there is Gaia as a way of viewing and understanding the world. To return to Lovelock and Margulis, they and I were Lindisfarne Fellows, members of the Lindisfarne Association founded by cultural historian and author, William Irwin Thompson. This was a gathering of scientists, artists, engineers, farmers, economists, political scientists, historians, spiritual teachers, philosophers, and even an astronaut. The men and women of the Fellowship were engaged in projects to promote a positive future for humanity based on a society committed to holistic thinking and behavior. They were, and still are, individuals working to bring a new way of seeing and being into the world. [If you would like to read the very interesting history of the Lindisfarne Fellowship, please see *Thinking Together At The Edge Of History*, by William Irwin Thompson, published by Lorian Press.]

Every year, the Fellowship held a conference in which the Fellows could get together and share ideas. At one of these conferences, the theme was "Gaia: A Way of Knowing," based in part on the Gaia Theory. Several of the talks at this conference were later collected into a book of the same title edited by William Irwin Thompson. Although it was published thirty years ago, the ideas it contains are still very relevant; it remains available on Amazon.com.

The conference focused on "Gaia" as not only referring to the planet as a living organism but also as a new epistemology. Gaia represented a new way of perceiving and thinking about the world, a holistic, ecological, systems-oriented world view. It is a way of understanding the world as networks and patterns of synergic relationships creating a whole, rather than as a collection of discrete but separate and unrelated entities. As it states on the dust jacket of the book *Gaia: A Way of Knowing*, when all the elements of this new way of knowing "are looked at together, what can be seen is the foundation of a startling new paradigm of wholeness: life as cognition, communication, knowing."

Of course, this is from a human point of view. This way of knowing is new to us, at least in our Western culture. But if Gaia is indeed a planetary organism, a World Soul, then such a holistic perspective is natural to it. It's how an organism that is responsible for sustaining and nurturing the complex interactions that make up the ecology of the planet would think. Further, to such a planetary intelligence, all things are alive. Whether they exist in material, physical form or in a subtle, non-physical form is irrelevant; both are part of the wholeness of the planet.

When we understand this, and begin to adopt this worldview and way of thinking, then we are "thinking like a planet." We are perceiving and engaging the world in ways that are holistic, ecological, and systemic: honoring the whole and the whole-within-the-part. It is a worldview that is native and instinctive to the non-physical beings who are my subtle colleagues, but it's one that's not so familiar yet to most of us living in the industrialized world, which is historically based on a non-holistic, non-ecological worldview. As we are seeing the destructive consequences of that approach, it seems to me the challenge of our time, for our survival and the survival of many other species that share the biosphere with us, is to learn how to "think like a planet." It is a form of thinking that is infused with love and the willingness to nourish and foster life in all its forms.

The art of Gaianeering is to *perceive* life, the world, and ourselves in a holistic, systemic, ecological, and "Gaian" way. We need to understand the world as a living system containing both physical and non-physical systems. After all, how we see the world is important. It informs and guides our choices and our actions.

For me, the Gaianeering worldview has four interwoven parts:

- Learning to think in ecological, holistic, and systemic ways.
- Recognizing the subtle half of the planet, Earth's "second ecology."
- Recognizing that life transcends biology and thus that everything is alive.
- Revisioning the role of humanity on the Earth.

Although each of these will be familiar to readers of this journal, I'd like to say more about each of them by way of emphasizing their importance.

<u>Holistic, Systemic Thinking:</u> Gaianeering involves seeing the world as an interconnected whole and thus thinking in ecological terms. This is more than just developing the kind of environmental awareness that is part of the first "Face" of Gaia. It means learning to think in terms of relationships, connections, and whole systems: in effect, appreciating the ways in which everything affects everything else. It is an appreciation of the dynamic interdependency of life.

The word *holism* was coined by Jan Smuts, a South African philosopher, general, and statesman, in his 1926 book *Holism and Evolution*. In it, he postulated a force in creation that created wholes which are more than just the sum of their parts, and that these wholes become parts of still greater wholes. To understand the world, one must see how things interconnect and form into wholes: an understanding at the heart of ecology.

Another description of this way of seeing the world is found in General Systems Theory. Although the basic concepts are ancient—it could be said, for instance, that the Chinese oracle, the *I Ching*, with its appreciation of the interconnectedness of things, is an early example of this approach—the modern presentation of these principles was developed and promoted by Ludwig van Bertalanffy, an Austrian biologist. His seminal book, *General Systems Theory*, published in 1968, became the foundation for the development of systems thinking in many fields, including science, economics, and cybernetics. Since then, many others have elaborated on his principles, adding their own insights in support of a holistic paradigm of how our world works.

The Subtle Worlds—Earth's Second Ecology: If we are going to have a holistic, systemic view of the world, then we cannot ignore the existence of the non-physical or "subtle" dimensions of the Earth. Unfortunately, once well known to our ancestors, knowledge of these dimensions is now obscured by fantasy, superstition, religious belief, fear, and materialism. Yet we all experience and participate in this subtle ecology in one way or another, even if we don't recognize it when we do. Though we may have lost awareness of this fact, we do not inhabit just the physical part of the planet: we inhabit the planet as a whole, including its subtle dimensions.

The existence of a subtle dimension to the world has been experienced by people for millennia, but it has not always been viewed as a natural, organic ecology with its own diverse environments and the various non-physical organisms (elementals, nature spirits, angels, Devas, non-physical humans, and so forth) that live within them. This ecology is very different in constitution than the material world with which we are familiar and follows natural laws that are suitable to its nature and thus equally different from those we know. Nevertheless, the basic principles of interconnectedness and interdependency that are at the heart of ecology are as true in the subtle worlds as they are in the physical. Equally true is the fact that this interdependency and interconnectedness extends between these two parts of Gaia. It is this wholeness of the world with which we must engage if we are to fulfill the promise of Gaianeering. This means taking the subtle worlds out of the realms of disbelief, superstition, magic, religion, and mysticism and learning to appreciate them and the beings within them as partners in a planetary ecosystem.

Everything is Alive: An essential part of a Gaian way of knowing is realizing that everything is alive. We divide the physical world into organic and inorganic parts, into that which is biological and alive and that which is not. Gaia makes no such distinction. The reason is that the subtle dimension is a dimension of life. All subtle energies are sentient and alive, and these energies are woven into the fabric of physical matter. "Organic" and "inorganic" are two subsets of our material ecology, but they are both manifestations of the larger planetary ecosystem which is alive.

My coffee cup is inarguably different from me. It is, on the physical level, a non-living object. But as a system of subtle energies, it is sentient and alive in a way that transcends terms like "organic" and "inorganic." If I relate to the whole energy field of my coffee cup—or of any other object—with love, appreciation, respect, and blessing, I will receive a reciprocal response. Outwardly, the coffee cup remains the same, but within the energy ecology of the subtle realm, its energy field surges in response to my own, and it becomes heightened in a way that would not happen if I ignored it.

The challenge we face as human beings is that we moderns think we dwell on a planet of things, and we treat the world accordingly, even reducing each other at times to the status of objects to be used and manipulated. The truth is that we live in a planet of beings, a planet of life, and until we fully appreciate this and act accordingly in a Gaianeering way, we will continue to run into difficulties as our worldview clashes with the reality of the world itself.

<u>Revisioning Humanity</u>: In a Gaian perspective, humanity does not stand separate and superior to the rest of nature and the planet. There is no "anthropo-exceptionalism." We are not special. The idea that we are, that we have a right to dominate the planet and to do what we wish with all other forms of life and existence, has had its day. It has demonstrably led us to the current state of environmental crisis that may even threaten our own existence. The idea that we can act upon nature any way we choose with no ill effects or consequences to ourselves is outmoded, inaccurate, and dangerous. There might have been a time when we were fewer in number and our technologies less impactful when we could get away with such a worldview, but this is no longer the case.

This would be true even if we were not faced with actual environmental dangers. Cooperation, collaboration, and partnering are more effective ways of getting things done than through domination, control, and conflict. If we want to be Gaianeers, we need to think in terms of relationship and symbiosis. It is love that will carry us into a more productive and creative state of human/Gaian relationship.

This means that if we are going to understand and adopt a Gaian way of knowing, we must stop seeing ourselves as separate from the world, working our will simply because we think we can get away with it. We can't get away with it any longer, nor should we want to. We need a new vision of humanity participating in the wholeness of the world and in the process, discovering our own wholeness as a species. We may not be special—all forms of life are special to themselves and to Gaia—but we are unique in the set of physical, mental, emotional, and spiritual qualities and capacities that we possess. The flowering of that uniqueness in self-discovery and unfoldment will come when we realize and embody our place in the whole and define ourselves accordingly.

Partnership (Gaia as World Soul)

The **third** Face of Gaia is that of the World Soul, a subtle being whose life energy envelops and pervades the planet. In esoteric traditions, Gaia is usually considered to be the Intelligence that supervises and empowers the evolution of life and consciousness on the Earth. Here, the art of Gaianeering is one of *partnership* and collaboration between ourselves and this planetary spirit, especially in responding and partnering with the field of the "New Gaia" I wrote of earlier.

But what does this mean? What or who is the World Soul? What kind of being is it with which we are partnering, and, for that matter, what does partnering mean? Further, as my subtle colleague said above, in some respects *we* are Gaia. What does this mean in a context of collaboration? Are we collaborating with ourselves?

I had my first contact with Gaia back in 1966, and my experience of it then was of a specific being, not unlike encountering Mother Nature. But as I gained more experience with the subtle worlds and with subtle beings, under the tutelage of my subtle colleague, John, I began to realize and appreciate just how complex and in some ways indescribable in words many subtle beings are, especially those operating on what might be called a "planetary" or "cosmic" wavelength. This includes Gaia.

I think of Gaia these days as a "diffused Individuality," something akin, I suppose, to the idea of a "center without circumference" or the holographic condition in which every part of a hologram contains the whole hologram. While we think of ourselves as having relationships and connections to the world around us, a being like Gaia *is* its relationships and connections. It is not without boundaries but the way these boundaries present themselves and function is different from the way boundaries manifest here in the physical plane. I could call Gaia a "planetary field," but it's a specific Identity as well, capable of personifying itself when needed.

One of my subtle colleagues once attempted to convey this idea by likening Gaia to a chicken from which chicken broth is made to produce a planetary soup. (I was probably hungry when he said this!) But in my understanding and experience of Gaia, he could as easily have said Gaia was a broth which could manifest as a chicken. The point is that both chicken and chicken broth point to the existence of something that nourishes and which allows very different elements to be blended together into a unique whole. Just what that something is may be beyond our ability to precisely define.

This time around, while writing this issue, one of my subtle colleagues—a different person than communicated with me in that previous issue of *Views*—had this to say about Gaia:

SC: When we graduate from the Post-Mortem Realm, we enter the world of multi-dimensionality. While we occupy time and space, we do so in a different way from you living in a three- and four-dimensional wavelength. What you may term the "higher realms" are those in which multi-dimensionality and thus complexity increase. While we continue to possess individuality, it is defined by factors different from what you usually look for on your level. I would not call our individuality "diffused," though I understand why you may do so; I would say our individuality is "extended." We are not all smeared together into an amorphous oneness, but we do participate in each other. You might say, therefore, we have "participatory individuality." You incarnate persons do, too, though you do not always recognize it.

As you know, we often appear to you as human individuals such as you would meet in your daily life; it's easier for you to relate to us in this manner. But with practice, you have also learned to commune with us in our multi-dimensional state in which our forms appear diffused while our identities are not.

This is true for Gaia who can appear to any of you in any number of forms which may facilitate contact. To try to define exactly what Gaia is, though, may well be futile for minds working in a three-dimensional context. Call it the World Soul and let it go at that for now.

However, it is important to understand that Gaia is a dynamic state, evolving as any Life does; it is constantly taking in streams of energy and information from the Lives that manifest as the sun, the other planets, and the stars. It also takes in such streams from the multitude of lives within its planetary sphere, both physical and non-physical, including human life, and from its own sacred Interiority. All of this must be processed and integrated. As conditions change, as lives evolve, as information streams grow more complex, then you might say Gaia needs greater processing power. This is achieved in one fundamental way: by increasing the density and complexity of its connections and the grace of the flow within them. Think of the formation of neurons in your own brain, and you will have, metaphorically, a picture.

The "Gaian Wave" or the expanding field of "New Gaia," as one of our colleagues phrased it, is bringing about this greater processing power. It is rewiring the world, so to speak. It does so by creating new connections both within the Gaian system and in its relationships to its stellar environment, but mostly it is doing so by enhancing the flow within connections already existing. You might say it is enhancing the efficiency of these connections. Of course, the fundamental power for this enhancement and rewiring is love.

Hence the pressure towards greater wholeness and communion. For humanity, the changes are obvious. Old patterns that foster separation and divisiveness must be broken up. There are changes in the subtle realms and thus changes in the nature—you might say in the architecture and wiring—of the human subtle body. Space and opportunity must exist for the arising of a Gaian individuality that honors the uniqueness of each incarnate identity yet creates new channels for individuals to collaborate with increasing care and support for each other. The object is the emergence of a new phase in human evolution, a Gaian humanity that becomes an active and conscious participant in the manifestation of Gaia's wholeness.

For this to be accomplished, you do not yet need to

fully understand the nature of Gaia, but you do need to understand your own nature to discover how you may enhance the "New Gaia"—which for you is a new human—and not resist it.

David: Can you tell me more of the difference between "Gaia" and "New Gaia," as you see it.

SC: In all essential ways, there is no difference. You may rewire your computer so that it can process information faster, but you are still doing the same tasks, though additional capacities may now become available due to the enhanced processing. Think of the new subtle energy field of Gaia as one in which love flows more fully and effectively, thus enabling greater collaboration. After all, if you have a team of people who improve their relationships, their communication, their interactions, their love and caring for each other, then their capacities as a team will be increased. Greater wholeness will manifest.

It is true that Gaia is reorganizing itself to better receive and hold what might be called advanced energy flows of life and spirit from the stellar realms and from the sacred. New information and energy are becoming available. But the need now at your level is to open and build the conscious connections of intention and love between you and the spirit of Gaia, as well as between you and all the others who share the world with you. In this way, you come into harmony with the new field and help to enhance its performance.

Over the years, I've learned that partnering with a subtle being means coming into resonance and harmony with what it does, that is, with its function. For instance, if I want to collaborate with the nature spirits in my back yard who work with the energy field and spirit of my maple tree, I offer what I can through love and blessing to nurture the life in that tree. I try to become energetically a nature spirit. If they are blessing the tree, then I'll bless the tree, too. If they are acting as conduits for living energies from Gaia to flow into the energy field of the tree, then I look for what spiritual energies I can attune to that I can pass on to the tree.

Partnering with Gaia and with the field of the "New Gaia" is no different in principle. The first thing I want to do is not to define what Gaia *is* but to define what Gaia *does*. What is its energetic function and how might I replicate it in some manner in my own life?

I see Gaia as performing the following functions, all of which are ultimately grounded in and expressive of love:

- It honors life and incarnation.
- It supports individuality, uniqueness, and diversity.
- It supports connection, collaboration, symbiosis, and synergy.
- It ensures that lines of evolution and growth are open and protected and thus that change and development are always possible.
- It maintains, empowers, and protects a circulatory flow of vitalizing life energy nurturing all beings within its influence.
- It maintains a process for recognizing, removing, or recycling forms, patterns, and energies that are toxic; like any organism, it has ways of removing "waste."
- It has ways of healing and redeeming broken and injured parts.
- It sustains processes for maintaining an evolving coherency, integration and wholeness.

- It builds and maintains connections and relationships with its own wider, cosmic and solar environments.
- It opens pathways for sacredness to emerge and express.

The art of Gaianeering involves seeing ourselves as partners with Gaia, helping in our human fashion to foster and empower the evolution of consciousness and life in our world. It means using our creative imagination and skills in ways that align with Gaia's intents as represented by the functions I listed above. It means aligning with and empowering the healthy flow of living energy throughout the dimensions of the world.

What would it mean, for instance, to conduct our affairs, to build our buildings, manage our agriculture, generate our energy, and engage in economic activity in ways that partner with Gaia and align with its functions? How can our engineering be Gaianeering?

One form of partnership with Gaia that has been receiving more and more attention in the past decade is subtle activism. This practice collaborates with the energizing, healing and restorative properties of the World Soul to provide blessing and energetic help to areas of distress and suffering anywhere on the planet. Subtle activism can also be used to empower positive actions and developments on the world scene. It is a skill that can be learned, a skill taught in several of Lorian's classes in working with subtle energies and with Gaia.

We have much to explore and learn in this area of Gaian collaboration and Gaianeering. It begins with recognizing the existence and reality of Gaia and seeing ourselves as its partners, not its children nor its stewards and certainly not as its dominators. Partnering is born of mutual respect, love, and a sense of what each can offer to the other. As I said earlier, this entails developing new ways of thinking about ourselves and about our world. If we manage to do so, we will be all the better for it.

Presence (Gaian Consciousness)

The **fourth** Face of Gaia is our own face when we act in blessing and support of the wellbeing of the planet and its wholeness. Then we become a *presence* of what could be called a "Gaian consciousness." We not only think like a planet, we act like one as well, giving expression in our own unique ways to the life-affirming and nurturing spirit of Gaia in the world. This is more than simply "thinking like a planet." It is "being a planet." It is expressing a "Gaian consciousness."

How do we do this?

It's not that difficult. Each of us holds a piece of Gaia within him or her. How could it be otherwise since we are part of the planet, physically and subtly? It's a matter of attuning to that part of us and bringing it forth in our actions.

When he was a young man, my father wanted to become a doctor and travel to Africa to work with Dr. Albert Schweitzer in his jungle clinic. This ambition didn't work out for him, but all his life, Dad was inspired by Schweitzer's credo of "Reverence for All Life." In every way he could, he sought to implement that spirit in his dealings with the world.

The spirit of Gaia is one of honoring, empowering, fostering, and nurturing life and consciousness. It's not only a spirit of reverence for life. It's a spirit of love as well.

This is a spirit that any of us can embody. Its simplest expression is to practice blessing as a way of relating to our world, greeting each person, each life, each thing with a radiance of goodwill and affirmation. What makes it a "Gaian" way of being—a Gaian consciousness—is that this reverence and kindness is for everything, remembering that to Gaia, everything is alive. Our blessings are for the objects around us as much as for the people and creatures whom we meet, since all things, organic and inorganic, are systems of sentient, living energy. This life may manifest more clearly on a subtle level of existence than in the material world, but it's still there. It will benefit from and even respond to acts of love and blessing.

Since we are subtle beings as well as physical ones, we can generate a Gaian vibration in our own subtle energy field that can radiate, like a "Gaian sun," its qualities into the subtle environment. Through meditation and attunement, we can align with the spiritual qualities of Gaia itself in ways that draw out and empower those same qualities in us. We really can be a Gaian presence, strengthening and enriching the evolutionary field of the "New Gaia" wherever we are.

There are deeper levels to exploring and embodying a Gaian consciousness. Here is a comment from the subtle colleague who spoke earlier:

> SC: I have said that energetically Gaia is rewiring itself, creating new patterns of energy flow, processing, and integration. This means that the subtle energy field of humanity is rewiring itself as well. Eventually, this will affect every individual person and how he or she as a soul enters into the incarnate realms to take embodiment in the world. A new kind of human being is emerging over time.
>
> Most of this rewiring and change is happening now in the subtle realms; it will not show up in the majority of incarnate humans for a while, but future generations of humans will have a new subtle body allowing them a deeper, more organic and intimate sense of connection and participation with the presence of Gaia. They will participate more fully in creating the new levels of

integration, collaboration, and wholeness the World Soul now requires within itself: the greater degree of "processing" that I spoke about.

If I could tell you exactly how this will manifest in incarnate humanity and when, I would, but this information is not available to me. Much depends on the choices you are all making now and their consequences. Much depends on how much openness or resistance there is to the changes that are unfolding within and around you. The process can move gracefully and quickly or it can be delayed with an increase in suffering and stress. It is why we are promoting this information to encourage as many of you as possible to respond in positive and helpful ways.

It is possible to take up a mantle of joy, love, and a positive embrace of your future. Your imagination of what can be will have a strong effect on what is, but remember that imagination is more than a mental process. It is more than just holding an image in your mind. It is holding the felt sense of a new reality in your whole being, from your body outwards into your subtle fields.

You teach this in your process of manifestation and the idea of the "New You." It is the same principle. You can hold in yourself a Gaian New You and thus a "New Gaia," as I have said. Doing so is an act of joy, not fear or despair. It is an act of hope, which is not wishful thinking but a power to open the door to possibilities.

For those of you who begin to open to the field of the "New Gaia" in this way, your own subtle bodies will begin to change and repattern themselves. This is not a far future phenomenon but something that is occurring now in the subtle worlds and can also occur in the lives of those incarnate who are open to the possibility.

Towards this end, I give you my blessings.

Exploring this idea of a "new subtle body," what it may be like, and how we can help bring it into being is the theme for future exploration. Researching this is very much a work in progress, but whoever or whatever *Homo Gaian* may be, I am sure that the art of Gaianeering is an avenue of its emergence.

Being A Gaianeer (Putting It All Together)

Gaianeering is a practice that combines and blends Participation, Perception, Partnership, and Presence. How these are combined depends on the individual. One person may find that participating in and contributing to one or more of the various "Green" efforts to protect and heal our physical ecology is their focus. Another may focus on subtle activism as a form of partnering. For someone else, it may be exploring just what a Gaian consciousness entails and how to embody it. If you wish to be a Gaianeer, then find which of these four "Faces" of Gaia is where you'd like to start and pursue it.

What you will find as you do, though, is that all these four approaches depend on each other. To Participate well, you need Perception, Partnership, and Presence. To be a Gaian Presence, you need to Participate, Partner, and Perceive and think like a planet. You may start with one "Face," but inevitably you will be led to the others, for Gaianeering is a whole approach that puts them all together.

When you realize this, you also realize that Gaianeering points to the fulness of what it means to be a human being upon the Earth and within the community of Gaian life. It points to our wholeness.

In truth, Gaia has only one Face, and that is the Face of active love and service to the unfoldment and betterment of life on Earth in all its forms.

To be a Gaianeer is to make that Face your own.

CHAPTER FOUR
Issue 26, December 2017

The Christ Event

Knowing that this issue would come out in December, I wanted to use it as an opportunity to explore that planetary phenomenon which I think of as "the Christ Event." Although associated with the birth of Jesus and the rise of Christianity, the Christ Event is much more, transcending a particular person or a particular religion and the institutions to which it has given birth.

The word "Event" may be misleading here as it can suggest something happening at a specific moment in time, something with a beginning and an ending. We might think that the Christ Event is coterminous with the life of Jesus or, even more specifically, with the three years of his teaching between his baptism by John and his crucifixion on the cross. However, I use the term to suggest a spiritual event as seen by my colleagues in the subtle realms. From their perspective, the Christ Event is still happening, not as an effect or consequence of the life and teaching of Jesus but as an activity extending back into the ancient origin of our planet and unfolding itself right now in the present and into the foreseeable future.

This perspective is born of a different experience of time. Whereas we see time as linear, my subtle colleagues tend to see it as a kind of foam filled with bubbles, much like you see around you if you take a bubble bath. I'm not at all sure I can adequately describe this, but where we see specific events, they see relationships, influences, and patterns of connections that form a distinct field that is more spatial than temporal in nature.

So, for instance, I see my life as a linear series of events from my birth to the present moment. But through their eyes, my life is a single event, the "David Event," like a bubble or sphere of activity and potential that is a coherent whole. It's like a round orange which, as it manifests in our time and space, is sliced into specific events. They see the whole orange, but we see the slices which are laid out on the table in a linear fashion.

This does not imply predestination or foreknowledge of the future. The nature and depth of the "slice" cannot always be predetermined. What was expected to be a "thin slice" containing a simple sequence of activities in the incarnate world ends up being a thicker slice due to unexpected complications or unforeseen but serendipitous connections. The "orange" remains the same but the manner of its slicing changes.

Likewise, the "orange" (in this example, of the "David Event") contains seeds which only sprout in the soil of earthly incarnation. However, how they sprout depends on the nature and condition of that soil at the time they appear. In other words, my subtle colleagues (and my own soul, for that matter) can look at the "orange" of my incarnation and see clearly the seeds within it, the intentions and potentials which my incarnation is designed to unfold and manifest. What they cannot see, what no one can see, is exactly which of these seeds will fall on fertile ground and which on barren ground, which seeds will give birth to healthy orange trees, and which will not for one reason or another. They (and I, as a soul) can be sure up to a point what will manifest, given what is known about the seeds and the soil, just like a farmer can more or less predict how her orange tree farm will turn out, but this knowledge is not absolute. Changes are possible. New discoveries are possible. Mutations in the seeds are possible, allowing unexpected flavors of orange to appear.

My point is that what we perceive as a series of linear events seemingly linked by chains of cause and effect and stretching from "the past" to "the present" and potentially into "the future," can be seen in the subtle worlds as a single, integrated, coherent, "bubble-like" Event containing multiple possibilities and potentials for unfoldment but also united by a single identity. After all, no matter how I slice my orange, it's still an orange and not an apple or an avocado.

In this picture, the physical plane with its form of time and space is like a great slicer that cuts these "orange-events" into a series of slices. We call the smaller slices at either end of the orange the "past" and the "future" and the large slice from the middle of the "orange" the "present." We look at the first slice and say, "This is the beginning. That is the event that started it all." Then we look at all the other slices and see them as consequences and effects when in fact, from the standpoint of the subtle realms, they are all the "beginning" and they are all "the present," and they are all "the future" because they are all part of a single coherent Event that transcends time and space.

This is the nature of the Christ Event for me. It is a huge planetary "orange" which is still being sliced by the knife of physical time and space. It is happening right now within us and around us. We are inhabiting one of the "slices."

The interesting thing for me is that the incarnation and life of Jesus isn't the first "slice." It's not even close to the beginning of this Event. If so, then what is the beginning of the Christ Event? Where and how does it first interact with the physical world, and what is the nature of that interaction?

To discover this, I first have to understand what the "orange" is.

The Orange

The Christ Event is "sliced" by incarnate human beings who align with its impulse, interpret its meaning, and manifest its spirit in their earthly lives to the best of their ability. This "slicing" is not necessarily done exclusively within the confines of Christianity. Although identified historically with Jesus and with all that stemmed from his life, the Christ "orange" has been and is being sliced and embodied by people in many cultures and religions. It is not dependent upon a particular name or upon affiliation with a particular set of traditions, teachings, and organizations, any more than the embodiment of love and goodwill is the exclusive province of one group of humans.

In the subtle worlds, the Christ "orange" is served by innumerable beings of all kinds, chief among whom are members of the angelic stream of evolution as well as many human souls active in the subtle dimensions. Some of my Pit Crew have a long association in different incarnations with service to this planetary "Event." It was to them that I turned for assistance in my research for this issue of *Views*. Interestingly, their first act was to mediate a contact with an angelic source deeply engaged with the implementation of the Christ Event. "You should hear what it has to say," they said. "It is a different perspective than you are used to hearing."

Contacting this angel was not easy. Unlike other angelic beings I've contacted over the years who have a close involvement with humankind and planetary evolution, this one seemed to exist and work far from the physical world. Even with help from my subtle colleagues—my "Pit Crew"—it took many days for my energy field to attune to this celestial being. It was limited in how far it could step its power and consciousness down to accommodate me, and I had to go deep into my soul to find the means to raise my own consciousness to where we could connect. When at last we came into resonance together, I found myself greeted and held by a graceful, even gentle, and loving presence.

The contact was very brief, but I felt as if a library-full of information was "downloaded" into my consciousness. I knew that it would take me days or weeks to unpack it all, not to mention the time needed to comprehend it. However, there was one communication that came through very clearly. What this angel said was this:

> You see the Christ as a divine impulse for the benefit and evolution, even the redemption, of humanity. We see it as the evolution of the consciousness and energy of love itself. It is Love coming to know itself in a new way.

I found this a stunning statement. I had never thought of love itself evolving. Upon reflection, though, I could understand it, at least in part. Beings evolve. Why not sacred qualities, which could be seen as Intelligences and Presences in their own right? Everything evolves, unfolding innate potentials. The cosmos itself is a means of self-discovery and unfoldment for the Generative Mystery that I call the Sacred. Who is to say that Love is perfect right from the get-go when creation emerges from the Unmanifest? Why should it not explore what it is capable of in an infinite variety of circumstances? To encounter an example of Love engaging in its own evolution should not have surprised me, but it did. I simply had never thought of it in that way before, though the angel seemed to regard it as perfectly natural.

Further, this perspective indeed offered a different way of thinking about the Christ. Rather than a divine savior incarnating for the salvation of humankind or a cosmic consciousness coming to boost the evolution of humanity, the emphasis here was on an act of self-discovery. It was the sacred quality of Love using the unique incarnational opportunities of the Earth, of Gaia, to deepen its ability to manifest in the manifest universe. In effect, Earth and all the lives upon it were acting over millennia as a creche—a manger—for the birth of a new expression of Love within the cosmos. That a new kind of humanity filled with this love might also evolve and bring its blessings into creation was wonderful—and a result much to be desired—but it was not, from this angel's point of view at least, the primary object of the exercise.

As a result of this experience, I realized that the Christ Event was a different kind of "orange" than I had thought it to be. Humanity was not at its center—nor was any other species of being, incarnate or not. I have to admit it felt a bit like discovering that the sun did not revolve around the Earth! Paradoxically, though, by shifting the emphasis of this Event from humanity to the evolution of Love itself as a fundamental divine quality—by "de-humanizing" it—I found I was able to feel the life and power of the Christ even more deeply and powerfully than I had before.

Not long after my angelic contact, one of my subtle colleagues came forward to remark on my experience.

> My Subtle Colleague (MSC): What the angel had to say to you is not unknown to us. It is something we could have shared with you, but it was important for you to experience this insight coming from its source. It does not negate the power and importance of the Christ in the context of human evolution, but it gives a deeper picture of the nature of both planetary and human involvement in this Event. You are less someone who needs rescuing and redemption and more someone who is a vital partner—though not the

only one—in a sacred act. Humanity is privileged to help bring Love into a new understanding of itself.

It must be said, though, that the Christ is a Mystery; it is a complex Event. The angel sees it from one perspective because it is an angel of Love whose job is to nurture that quality as it unfolds within creation. We see the Christ Event from a different perspective. We see it as the transmission of a pattern of being, a way of working with Love to bring it to fruition. These two points of view are not so far apart, but neither are they identical.

Think of it this way. You are given flowers to nourish in a garden. Bringing these flowers into bloom is the purpose of the garden. Think of this as the Flower Event. But along comes a master gardener who gives you insights into the nature of soil and seed and teaches you ways of husbandry that will help your flowers bloom even brighter. You could see the master gardener as an expression of the Flower Event as well.

The angel is attuned to the living spirit of divinity manifested in the presence of love. We are attuned to the gardener who teaches ways of working with that spirit to heighten its expression. Our emphasis is different, but we are both servants of Love.

After this, I wanted to reflect on this experience and compare it to experiences I had already had over the years of tuning in to the energy of the Christ Event. I realized as I thought about it that there were a number of threads now coming together for me, providing new depths to things I felt I already knew.

For instance, two years ago, I had been told by my Sidhe contact, Mariel, that Gaia was "the incarnation of a star." She had gone on to say that "As physical stars are the wombs of matter, so the stars of spirit are wombs of life. They are the matrix from which planetary spirits [like Gaia] emerge." At the time, one of my subtle colleagues had had to say about this:

> SC: Just as your sun generates and radiates energy in the form of waves and particles of light, so Gaia is a stellar being that generates and radiates energy in the form of waves and particles of life. All the beings upon the earth are like rays of energy and Light. You are a "photon" of life, and humanity is collectively a wave of life.
>
> Are all planets incarnations of stellar beings? No. Are all planets with life incarnations of stellar beings? No. But Gaia is, and this is what gives your world such a rich diversity of life-forms. But even this is not fully what distinguishes your Planetary Spirit as the embodiment of a stellar being. Here we touch on a mystery that is central to your human experience.
>
> Gaia is a stellar being who is incarnating the qualities of the stellar realm into the physical realm for its blessing and transformation. In a sense, one of the highest of living frequencies is reaching down to become one with one of the lower frequencies of being. It is a great experiment, one involving more than just the human species but certainly one that affects your own destiny. In particular, it is nurturing the arising of forms of life and consciousness that can embody, hold, and express the generative qualities and capabilities of the stellar realms. It is an experiment in transmitting and implanting aspects of its own nature into life-forms in both the subtle and the physical realms, creating as it were organic stars.

Though I certainly had not thought of what my subtle

colleague said back then in terms of the Christ Event, it sounded very similar to what the angelic contact had said. More to the point, the feeling—the felt sense—behind the words and images was much the same, as if both beings were describing the same event from two different perspectives.

My understanding of the physical dimension from my work with Incarnational Spirituality is that it is a place of intensity. Physical matter holds consciousness within boundaries that are harder and less permeable than what exists in the subtle worlds. It creates an experience of separation that often requires an act of will to overcome, to go beyond these boundaries to form connections. It also creates what I might call "communities of difference," in which we are brought together in the physical environment with people whose energy and consciousnesses are different from our own. This is different from my experience of the subtle worlds where, under most circumstances, people are brought together through resonance, creating "communities of harmony."

This is a simplification, but a helpful one, I think, to understand some of the challenges that a soul faces when it incarnates and finds itself having to deal with difference in ways it has not faced in the subtle environments. Not that there are not forces of resonance and similarity pulling us together with people who are like ourselves, but in the main, to progress in this world, we have to learn to work and hopefully create harmony with those who are not like us. Compared to the subtle worlds where the sense of an underlying unity and connectedness is strong, in the physical world, it is the differences that are emphasized by the very structure of matter. More often than not, we need to be intentional about making connections and creating harmony, even with those to whom we feel attracted and loving.

The point is that in the physical dimension, Gaia has manifested a gym for the soul, a place to exercise "muscle groups" of will and love. Wholeness doesn't manifest automatically. We have to work at it and feel what it means to create it. From the soul's point of view, this gives us deeper insights into what wholeness is and how it is created and the role that love plays in this process.

In the words of my subtle colleague from two years ago, Gaia nurtures "the arising of forms of life and consciousness that can embody, hold, and express the generative qualities and capabilities of the stellar realms." From the point of view of the angel, Gaia also nurtures the spirit of Love as a sacred quality. It creates an environment in which love itself as a living force can evolve. To the angel, this is the Christ Event.

But is it all of it? Is it the whole orange?

Boundary

I have found over the years that in dealing with concepts transmitted from the subtle worlds, especially from those multi-dimensional realms that are the homes of souls and angels, nothing is ever simple. You follow one thread of thought, and a dozen more appear leading in different but ultimately related directions. It's easy to get lost, the subtle world equivalent of "going down the rabbit hole" on the Internet.

At such moments, one looks for landmarks for orientation and direction. The landmark that stood out for me was the concept of *Boundary*.

Boundary can be understood in so many ways. Boundaries can be permeable membranes or stout and hard walls. They can be thresholds defining one region from another. They can be chasms separating one place from another. They divide, but they also provide meeting places.

The cyberneticist Gregory Bateson once said to me in a conversation, "Boundaries are where all the exciting things happen." As a biologist, I had to agree with him. Perceptions occur at boundaries; changes and evolution occur at boundaries. Creativity happens at boundaries.

I've long felt that the universe itself came into being out of an act of creating a boundary: the threshold or membrane between the mysterious Unmanifest and the Manifest cosmos that emerges from it.

One of the characteristics of a boundary is that it creates a resistance. It blocks or diverts something. It causes a change in direction. It is a "no" in the midst of a "yes."

It seems to me that without such resistance, without a "no" as well as a "yes," creativity is not possible. If I'm writing a book, I have to say yes to its content but no to everything that is extraneous or distracting from that content. If I'm creating a universe, I have to say "no" in some manner to the Unmanifest state in order for manifestation to come into being. I have to say, "Unmanifestness goes no further; beyond this boundary, this threshold, this membrane, this creative intention, it is the Manifest that, well, manifests."

When we think of a boundary, we often think of what is being excluded. What is the boundary saying "no" to? But a boundary also says "yes" to what happens within the dedicated and protected space that it creates. A cell membrane protects the cell from its environment even while enabling the cell to engage with that environment; at the same time, it encloses and holds the body of the cell: the nucleus, the organelles, the cytoplasm, the proteins that govern its metabolism. The membrane makes the life of the cell possible.

This points out an important function of boundaries: they make it possible to hold something. Boundaries create containers in which something can happen.

I think of a pressure cooker. Here food is cooked by heat generated by steam pressure. For this to work, though, the walls of the pressure cooker have to be strong enough to contain that pressure. I wouldn't buy a pressure cooker just for its walls; I buy it for what happens within those walls, the kind of cooking it makes possible. But I understand that the walls have to be sturdy and well-built to enable that cooking to take place.

What is important here is to appreciate that a boundary says no to something but at the same time, it says yes to something else. And sometimes the nature of the "no" makes possible an emphasis on the "yes," as with my pressure cooker.

There is another function of Boundary. It makes relationship possible. In our universe, everything proceeds from relationship. Relationships generate energy, power, growth, and emergence. According to many quantum physicists, at the very root of matter lies not another, ultimate subatomic particle but a dynamic flux of relationships.

Relationship demands the existence of an Other. It requires that which is different from oneself, something with which or with whom to form the relationship. Boundaries, membranes, thresholds all create this difference, making relationship possible. This is why I think of the first act from which creation emerged to be the establishing of a boundary of some mysterious nature between the Unmanifest and the Manifest. It is the creation of a "yes" and a "no" that makes everything that follows possible.

The "orange" of the Christ Event is all about love, whether it's the evolution of love itself as a living quality of divinity, as the angel described to me, or it's the manifestation of love as a holopoietic force—a wholeness-creating, connective force—within the world. In either case, though, boundary is important. Boundary as a phenomenon creating relationship is what makes the Christ Event possible. It's why I think of it as a landmark to help me navigate through the complexity of concepts and images that surround me at times as I tune into this great planetary "orange."

To understand this, I come back to a difference I experience between the physical and subtle worlds. It could be symbolized (and it *is* just a symbol, not the full reality of it) by the oft-used image from quantum physics that light is both a particle and a wave. That is, from one perspective, photons act as if they have boundaries and are particles, while from another perspective, they act as if they don't, as if they are one continuous presence, a wave.

The subtle worlds are not without boundaries—and some of them can be impenetrable if you don't know how to pass them or have the means to do so. However, compared to the physical realm, they seem more wave-like. As I said earlier, the underlying sense of connectedness and flow is very strong; it doesn't sweep away individuality but it embeds it and defines it in participation in a larger unity of life, like a fish within the ocean. By contrast, as we can see in our everyday experience as incarnate individuals, the physical world is very particulate. You and I might feel love for each other but at the same time, we know our separateness as two unique persons, two human "particles."

If I am a flowing, universal quality like love and I want to deepen my understanding of myself and access potential new capacities, how might I go about it? How might I "cook" myself in an evolutionary way?

A pressure cooker might not be a bad idea.

It just so happens that Gaia has one. A lot of them, in fact. They are all manifestations of incarnate life, whether mineral life, plant, animal, or human. The nature of incarnate life in our world is that it takes place within boundaries, forcing us to form relationships differently than we do in the subtle, non-physical dimensions. We learn about expressing love in ways not so possible in the subtle worlds. Might this not be true for Love as well as a living aspect of the Divine? Might this not be part of the Sacred's own self-discovery?

There are mysteries here, and I don't pretend to grasp them. However, I do know from my studies what the material, physical realm has to offer because of the way in which boundaries manifest here and the form holding takes. If I were a flowing, universal quality, this is the place to come to learn, though the particulate pressure cooker, how to unfold undiscovered aspects of myself. It is a place of "no's" that enable me to better understand and express my "yes's."

When we think of the Christ Event, it is not uncommon to think of it as love incarnating into the world; after all, love is one of the ways we define Christ Consciousness. When we do so, we are likely imagining love as a presence—most likely in the form of a being such as Jesus—come to redeem, heal, inspire, and bless humanity and the Earth. Love is an already formed quality doing its thing on Earth, like sunshine giving light and warmth to the planet. It incarnates into the world as an act of service, even, in some traditions, of sacrifice. But from this angel's point of view, Love is also incarnating into the Earth for its own development. Love is incarnating—entering into the world—for its own sake, not to "save" humanity or to be a force advancing the evolution of the Earth. Is one view more correct than another?

Again, my subtle colleagues had comments to make.

> MSC: This is not a matter of "either/or." It rarely is when dealing with matters of complexity arising from the highest realms of beingness. Truth lies in paradox, not in

one side or another.

Think of what the angel said through the lens of Incarnational Spirituality. Each person incarnates into the world for the sake of their soul and its evolution, yet they also are participants in and hopefully contributors to the life and wholeness of the world. Further, the incarnate self is not unaccompanied but is companioned by the presence and Light of its Soul.

Shall not the same be true for Love? It may seek new depths and understandings of its own nature within the Divine ecology of being, but its presence in the world cannot help but be a blessing and a service to the evolution of what is around it. Surely, like you, it can handle two tasks at once?

Likewise, it does not incarnate unattended. The angel with whom you spoke is an example of this, for it is one of Love's attendants, what you would call its "Pit Crew." But at the same time, it is accompanied by planetary, solar, and even stellar beings who shepherd its incarnational process, embodying and manifesting the quality of love in their own presence just as your soul manifests the presence of your sacred Identity in the midst of your earthly life.

The Christ Event encompasses all of this. Just like your incarnation, it is a complex ecology of consciousness and energy. It is not one thing exclusively or another but a drama through which love enhances its presence in the cosmos. It is taking advantage of an opportunity provided by the World Soul of this planet while at the same time contributing to the overall success of that which Gaia seeks to accomplish.

Is this not, then, the purpose and wonder of incarnation, no matter who or what is doing the incarnating?

A Partnership

This brings me back to the similarity between the experience I had with this angel and the message I had two years ago about Gaia being the incarnation of a star. In the latter, I was informed that "Gaia is a stellar being who is incarnating the qualities of the stellar realm into the physical realm" for the blessing and transformation of the latter. It was an "experiment" of blending two very different modes of being and energy to give rise to forms of life and consciousness that can embody, hold, and express the generative qualities and capabilities of the stellar realms."

To perform this "experiment," Gaia was intending to use the "pressure cooker" nature of the Holding and Boundary functions of the physical realm to "bake" the stellar qualities of consciousness into incarnate consciousness, producing, as my subtle colleague said at the time, "organic stars."

Is this experiment the same as the "evolution of Love itself" to which the angel was referring as the Christ Event? No, but the two are related. How they are related is part of the information I downloaded from that angelic contact.

There are two things to keep in mind about what Gaia was (and is) seeking to accomplish. The first is that the stellar realms are themselves rich and vibrant with the radiance of Love. Although I understand them as realms dedicated to the divine quality of Life itself, Love is an integral part of that quality. Therefore, the induction of a stellar quality of consciousness into a consciousness arising out of physical matter is in its own way an incarnation of love. Love is essential to the success of this experiment.

The reason this is so is the second thing we need to keep in mind. Because of the nature of how it expresses the functions of Boundary and Holding, physical reality creates a condition of intensity and pressure upon consciousness. On the one hand, this can accelerate the unfoldment of whatever innate capacities a particular "line" or "species" of consciousness might have, forcing it to deal with awareness and intention with the resistances—the "no's"—inherent in the nature of physical boundaries in order to arrive at the "yes's" that are equally possible.

As I said, energy and power flow out of relationships. Where intentionality is required to overcome boundaries to form those relationships, the energy that results is enhanced—not necessarily out of the relationships themselves but within the power of the "relationship-forming ability" of the consciousness itself.

However, the nature of these boundaries enhances the experience of separation, which can work against the forming of relationships. If the incarnating consciousness is not clear or strong enough to muster the required intentionality to overcome the resistances of the boundaries, then isolation can result, which makes the sense of separation stronger.

In other words, the experiment carries risks.

To minimize this risk, the quality of love needed to be part of the process. Therefore, as I understand it, whether there was a Christ Event or not, there would still be a necessary influx of love, coming both from Gaia and from its allies in the lunar, solar, and stellar realms.

The image that comes to my mind about this is baking bread. If I want the bread to rise, I have to introduce yeast into the process. In Gaia's experiment, love is the yeast.

But suppose the yeast itself explored and deepened into its own "yeastiness" in the process of participating in the baking of the bread? Now you would end up with risen bread and evolved yeast.

This is not going to happen with real yeast and bread, but as I understand it, this is exactly what is happening between the "rising bread" of Gaia and the "yeast" of the Love held within the Christ Event. Given what Gaia as the Planetary Soul wished to do, it also provided an opportunity for the consciousness of Love itself (if I may describe it in this way) to enter into the intensity of the "pressure cooker" Gaia was manifesting and use that process for its own discovery and deepening. How, exactly, would Love manifest in a realm of separation?

(This is, by the way, rendering a complex spiritual event in simplistic human terms, but hopefully it conveys a sense of the exploration and learning that was desired.)

In this way, a partnership was formed between Gaia and the sacred attribute of Love itself. The Christ Event (as understood by the angel) became part of Gaia's planetary experiment and evolution right from the beginning. This was the "first slice," which created the foundation for the Christ Event as understood by humanity to take place many millennia later.

The Double Helix of Christ

Out of the material which the angel presented (though it may be more accurate to say out of the material which I absorbed like a sponge through being immersed in its presence; it wasn't as if we were having an extended conversation in the way humans do together), I came away with a sense of how the Christ Event as the incarnation of Love interacted and intersected with planetary evolution over the course of uncounted millennia, going back before the appearance of organic life. In the terms of the metaphor I've been using, I had a sense of some, at least, of the different ways the orange has been sliced.

At the same time, as I was digesting and assimilating this material, there was information being presented to me by one or two of my subtle colleagues who are close to the Christ Event as seen through the lens of human evolution. They provided a kind of counterpoint adding nuance and balance to what the angel had presented. Their emphasis was on the Gaian—and later the human—side of this Event.

Here is what one of them had to say about this:

MSC: You need to understand what Gaia is doing. It is extending and holding a field of beingness from the stellar realms into the physical dimension. This creates a complex ecology of Light and Life attractive to a wide variety of consciousnesses with an equally wide set of evolutionary agendas.

You might think of it this way. If you have a single musician in a theater, songs composed for her will necessarily be tailored to what one person with one instrument can do. Many composers, looking for places where their music can be played, with pass her theater by. But if this musician is now part of a symphony orchestra, the number and complexity of songs that can be played is increased by magnitudes. Now many more composers of all different styles of music will seek out this orchestra to play their music.

Many planets support life and evolution but most do not do so within the vibrational range occupied by the physical universe. They are subtle planets filled with life, but they would appear as dead planets to you, barren of life, if you encounter them in the physical dimension. The "dimensional instruments" which such worlds provide are limited, sometimes to a single plane of being. A being such as Gaia, however, is providing a field for the evolution of consciousness within physical life. This provides an extremely attractive opportunity. Many different kinds of beings from the subtle dimensions will seek this world out to play the music of their evolutionary composition.

These evolutionary streams are provided by Gaia with helpers. These are beings who do not enter directly into whatever incarnational or evolutionary process those whom they shepherd or guard have selected or, in some cases, they are the successful graduates of such processes. They stand by to help and to guide from the outside and, if necessary, because of the risks physical incarnation can entail, to provide rescue or aid. They are all, in their way, servants of Love whose mission is to ensure that in the intensity and challenge of physical or etheric embodiment, things do not go awry.

We see these beings as serving the Christ Event that is part of Gaia. In the long term, if not always in the short term, the maintain the wholeness and balance of Gaia as the Planetary Spirit conducts its experiment.

Understand that the Intelligence and Presence of Love itself is engaged with Gaia as well and often contributes its blessing to those who are evolving within the ecology of Light that Gaia provides. Likewise, many of the Gaian helpers assist in the evolutionary deepening of Love as a sacred presence. The two sides of the Christ Event are not separate from each other but interweave even as they pursue different objectives. They are symbiotic.

However, the presence of the Christ Event as the evolution of Love itself can at times heighten and intensify the incarnational challenge of the Earth. It uses all those who evolve within the planet as the means of its own evolution. As they use love to solve the problems that Gaian incarnation can generate, they become instruments of exploration into the depths of Love itself. This means that there is a strong impulse within the Gaian ecology of beingness not merely to understand and use love as a tool but to be Love as a Presence.

It's as if at a music school, a student not only had to learn how to play his instrument well but also felt pressure to become music itself.

Not all beings in the history of the world have responded to this impulse or have even felt it, but those who have—and those who do now--experience a rare opportunity to accelerate their evolution into a whole new order of being. This evolutionary possibility is also part of the Christ Event, and it is particularly present in the human dimension of it.

Paradoxically, the presence of this evolutionary opportunity has increased the intensity of the incarnational experience in this world—not just now in the times in which you are living but throughout the millennia-long existence of the Earth. This in turn has generated resistance and at times opposition. The presence of the evolution of Love itself has at times given rise to its opposite in the form of hatred and rejection of what this Presence offers.

Therefore, at times there have been those who have come forward carrying the Light of Love as servants of Gaia to protect and defend and to confront and transforms those forces born from the imbalances the presence of Love itself can cause. These are the Christed beings with whom you are familiar and those of whom you have never heard nor would, from a human perspective, comprehend. Yet all are also part of the Christ Event.

To be the Grail in which Love discovers itself is a burden that Gaia has taken on, even beyond what it originally intended, yet it is an honor as well. It is this that makes this world a sacred planet.

In describing these two perspectives, which I'm calling the "Gaian" and the "angelic" Christ Events, I hope I don't give an impression that they are in any way competitive. As my subtle colleagues said, they are both interactive parts of an "ecology of Light," parts of a larger whole. Thinking of them, they seem to me like the two halves of the spiraling double helix of DNA. They mark the birth of the consciousness of Love in our world, or, if you wish, the birth of the Christ Within.

Pushmi Pullyu

When I was a child, I loved the Dr. Doolittle books by Hugh Lofting. These are the stories of a medical doctor who could talk to animals. He would travel all over the world, even to the moon, having amazing adventures and meeting wonderful creatures, with all of whom he could converse. I was envious! Talking with animals seemed like the most fun and useful talent that one could have.

In his adventures, he encounters a creature descended from a mating between a gazelle and a unicorn that has a neck and head at both ends of its body. It's called a "pushmi pullout." It's been sixty years since I last read one of the books, but as I recall, to move in one direction, this creature had to push from one end and pull from the other, hence the name.

The image of this creature came to mind as a result of further insights another of my subtle colleagues offered about the Christ Event.

> MSC: In your Christian tradition, the Earth is redeemed and sanctified by the incarnation of the Christ in the personage of Jesus. However, Love incarnated into the world at its earliest beginnings, making this an anointed or Christed planet from the outset, uncounted millennia before Jesus ever walked the earth or, for that matter, before any living organism appeared.
>
> As my colleagues said, this increased the pressure upon the incarnation of consciousness in this world which

has on occasion led to brokenness and the emergence of evil in different forms. But it has also meant that all beings who become part of the Gaian processes of life share and participate in this incarnation of Love and are blessed by it. Some are centrally involved, some only peripherally, but all are influenced by its presence in the fabric of the world. It is part of their spiritual DNA.

You could think of this presence as an arising Christ Event. It pushes life from within towards an expression and realization of Love in the depths of physical manifestation. At the same time, there is a pull upon consciousness coming from the higher levels of life, from avatars and other beings who are exemplars of the Sacred, embodiments of Love. They act to draw life towards its higher manifestations.

Thus, there is a push and a pull. There is a Christ Event thrusting upward out of life itself and out of the desire of Love to know itself. There is a Christ Event reaching downward, so to speak, using Love to assist the evolution of Gaian life in fulfillment of Gaia's intent. These two meet in humanity, both push and pull acting together to give expression to the sacredness of the Earth.

In other words, we are the pushmi pullyu of the Christ Event.

Sentiency, Self and Love

There are other insights about the Christ Event that have emerged for me while reflecting on my encounter with the angel.

In the Lorian Gaianeering conference of August 2017, Dr. Lee Irwin gave a talk on the subtle worlds. In it, he gave an excellent definition of *sentiency*. He said, "Sentiency is the impulse to form relationship." This exactly reflects my own experience of subtle energies, all of which, from my point of view, are both sentient and alive.

This "impulse to form relationship" implies awareness, but it seems to me it's an awareness that can function in much the way a tropism functions in a plant, like a flower turning towards the sun. It›s built into the structure, so to speak.

For example, I experience a living sentiency in the coffee cup sitting on my desk. If I send love to it, I can feel a pulse or "tendril" of subtle energy reaching back to me, seeking to form—as Lee says—a relationship with me. It is aware of the energy of love I have sent, and in that awareness, it senses me as the origin of that energy.

What I don't experience in my coffee cup, though, is consciousness. It is not aware of me if I'm not interacting energetically with it. It's not sitting on my desk thinking in a cup-ish way, "I wonder when David is going to pick me up?" It has no idea what a "David" or a human being is. Even when I interact with it energetically and send love in its direction, it's not responding to me as a human but to me as an energy source.

Consciousness, though, is more complex. It›s an awareness that encompasses other possible responses and engagements with the world beyond just a tropism towards wholeness. It seems to me there is a threshold—a «tipping point»—at which the complexity of the relationships formed through sentiency permit the emergence of consciousness. As consciousness itself develops in complexity, it gains the ability to hold and manifest the presence of Identity, which I see as a sacred attribute, which in turn can evolve into agency and self-consciousness.

I understand sentiency as being built into the structure of beingness as an expression of sacredness. In this context, love is an integral part of sentiency, for love makes relationship possible. In the Christ Event as described by the angel, Love incarnates into Gaia and in the process "quickens" or heightens the presence and action of Love in the sentiency of planetary matter. Now the impulse is not just towards relationship but towards relationships that create wholeness and therefore which reflect the holistic nature of the Sacred. Sentiency becomes infused with the property of *holopoiesis*— the impulse to create wholeness and in so doing to reveal sacredness in action.

In seeking to understand what the angel was showing me, I keep coming back to the idea that the Christ Event changes the nature of planetary matter from the very beginning, heightening its sentiency and thereby heightening its ability not only to manifest holopoietic relationships but also to receive and support complex energies of life. I interpret what I see as the world being infused with life (and this at a time long before physical life actually appeared). In seeing this, I can't help but remember what Jesus said in his expression of a Christ Event: "I come that they might have life and have it more abundantly." But it is not just life. It is a kind of life that can embody and manifest the presence of Love itself.

Seeing this brings me to a whole other realization. In entering into the "pressure cooker" of Gaia, Love encounters boundaries that reflect it back upon itself. Rather than the "steam of Love" escaping and dispersing, it is held in a way that intensifies it—the "pressure" grows—in a self-reflexive way. Love forms a relationship with itself; it becomes "self-sentient." Love becomes self-aware.

Yet, I'm aware that in thinking this, I'm sliding into anthropomorphism, using human terms and experience to try to explain something conveyed from a very non-human angelic perspective and consciousness. Understanding sits on the edge of my consciousness like a half-remembered dream. I might let it go, but I feel it's an important part of understanding the fullness of the Christ Event.

Love is what we think of as a quality. The angel sees it as much more than a quality. It is not a being, but it is a function, an Intelligence, a condition of sacredness that makes it possible for beings to exist.

Because it is not a being, it is not a "self," nor is it self-conscious. And yet, in the fire and intensity of Gaian incarnation—in the midst of the "pressure cooker"—it becomes self-sentient. It reflects back into itself and experiences itself as itself, not in relation to something else. It seems to me it becomes aware of its own divinity, and out of this awareness, a form of sentiency—or a way of forming relationships—becomes possible that was not possible before.

At this point (thankfully!), one of my subtle colleagues takes pity on me and my mental gyrations and steps forward to offer a comment.

> MSC: Think of love as a mode of divine consciousness. In what you call the "pressure cooker" of Gaia, it does not become aware of itself, for as you correctly perceive, it has no "self" as such of which to be aware—it is truly selfless. What it becomes aware of is the existence and nature of being within boundaries. It becomes aware of the bounded self and knows that this can be a manifestation of love as well. Do you understand? Love does not become a self, but "Self" as a divine phenomenon becomes Love. Selfhood becomes Love and vice versa. In the heart of Gaia, Love encounters Love in a way that gives it an understanding of Self. Individuality is sanctified and blessed.
>
> Is this not an understanding of the Incarnation? It is not that God has become human but that the Sacred has become Self in a particulate way, opening the door for

humanity to experience selfhood as a condition of love, not as a condition of separation.

You should not see this in temporal terms. I mean by this that this was not an evolutionary process. Love did not "learn" this over time. The moment Love enters Gaia as the angel describes, the seed of the sacred self emerges and becomes a possibility towards which earthly evolution may strive. Humanity is one expression of that striving.

You have often said that incarnation proceeds from an act of love, and by this, you meant out of a relationship of love between the soul and the world. This is true. But it is also true that at the very foundation of the experience of selfhood in this planet, there is Love knowing itself and revealing itself. It means that all incarnations are a manifestation of the evolution of Love, of Love knowing Self as a means through which it can express and not be lost. It is a reason that incarnation in your world is cherished and sought after.

All of this is reflected in the Christ Event as you customarily know it, focused on the life of Jesus. Where humanity errs is in seeing Love as the exclusive identity of one Self, the selfhood of Jesus. Like all beings of his stature and purpose, he incarnated not simply to teach you how to love, but to show you that you *are* Love and have been so since the foundation of the world.

From our position seemingly at the top of the evolutionary pyramid, we tend to see "self" as primarily a human attribute or at least we don't extend its presence very far down the evolutionary ladder. We may recognize it in some animals, but in our culture, we generally don't recognize it in what we call the "lower animals," insects, or in bacteria, much less in plants and in minerals. Yet the potential of the Sacred Self is there, too. From what the angel showed me, the "orange" of the Christ Event has been "sliced" in ways that embrace all these kingdoms of life as well. Christ as the incarnating presence of the sacred quality of Love has anointed all these lives and in its own way, has lived within them. I might not recognize or sense the Christ in the stone on my desk, but it is there, just as it is in the tiny insect crawling across my desk or the gardenia flowering a few feet from where I am sitting writing these words.

In human consciousness, though, this Love can truly flower in its self-awareness. We not only can love, we can be love.

It is this realization that the Christ Event focused around Jesus is intended to stimulate.

The Stellar Event

The mission of Gaia as a Planetary Soul emerging out of the stellar realms has been to give birth to a form of "organic, mobile star," a consciousness carrying the generative qualities of those realms and able to incarnate and serve anywhere within the subtle and physical realms. In keeping with the language I've been using, I could call this the "Stellar Event," which is "sliced" in its own way by its passage into and through physical spacetime.

I don't know exactly what qualities of life and beingness the stellar Intelligences wish to impart into evolving consciousnesses as their legacy from this process; this, I think, is what we are in the process of discovering in the course of human and planetary evolution, though it seems to me to be summed up in the phrase, "generative beingness." However, from what my inner colleagues have had to say, this consciousness needs to be anchored in an experience of the physical world or its equivalent. It's like an oceanographer who, in understanding the ocean, needs to experience diving to the deepest part of the seabed to know what those conditions are and what life exists there. It is Gaia's task to provide the means for that diving to take place.

While I hesitate to push this metaphor too far, we know that the only way our oceanographer can survive his time on the ocean floor is if she can be supplied with oxygen and an environment comparable to what she is used to on the surface. Given the "atmosphere" of love and life that exists in the stellar realms, the incarnating stellar qualities need access within the depths of physical and subtle world incarnation to the essence of that "atmosphere." Providing this is an expression of the Christ Event as well, the act of bringing Love—not as quality seeking its own self-discovery and evolution but as an active force manifesting the quality it already knows and possesses—into the depths of matter and into the evolutionary "ecology of Light" that Gaia provides.

There is a convergence of "Events" here within the Gaian planetary field, as indicated by the picture below. They are all taking advantage of the planetary "ecology of Light" that Gaia provides. They also interact with each other. This is particularly true of what I am calling the "Gaian Christ Event." This is the shepherding work of a variety of beings, human and non-human, using love in service both to the evolution of Love itself and to the progress and fulfillment of the "Stellar Event." Throughout millennia, up to the appearance of Jesus, there have been men and women (as well as "Christed" consciousnesses in the non-human evolutions) who have carried the energy of love and service to advance the spiritual evolution of life. The great philosophical and religious teachers who emerged during the Axial Age from the 8th to the 3rd centuries BCE can be seen as contributing to this

Gaian service by working to advance human consciousness.

This is an excellent example of the way many objectives can be served by the convergence and synergy of different agendas and purposes within the planetary field. To the extent that the Christ Event serves Gaia, it serves the Stellar agenda as well, even if not always directly. To use a previous metaphor, if we think of the Christ as yeast, then its presence allows several different kinds of bread loafs to rise simultaneously.

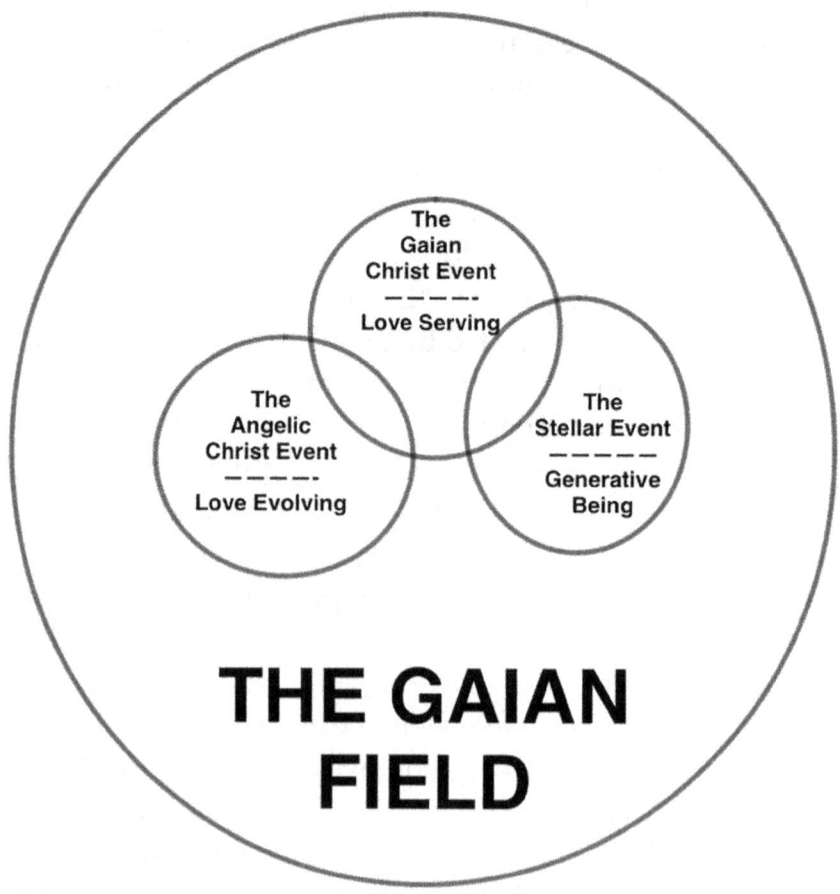

The life and mission of Jesus is part of the "Gaian Christ Event," but it also marks a place, as I said above, where the two "Christ Events" merge. For the first time, it became clear that a human being could be an incarnation of Love while also being an incarnation of Self.

We are still, two thousand years later, struggling to understand and embody this promise. Many people have experienced the "Selfhood of Love" and the "Christhood of Self," but for most of humanity, it remains a potential, if not a dream beyond our reach. Understanding the immediacy and even the ordinariness or naturalness of embodying the Christ Event in all its meanings is not easy to grasp, though it is what Incarnational Spirituality is about.

A New Subtle Body

What adds to the importance of our moment in history is that this is also a time when the third "Event," the "Stellar Event," is coming into embodiment. Within the Gaian Field, the three Events are beginning to merge. Much of the challenge we are facing in our time is due to the stresses and the rising potentials and opportunities created by this merging.

For many years, my subtle colleagues have said that the planet's subtle field is undergoing a transformation in order to accommodate the subtle and spiritual energies arising from the intersection of these three "Events." In the process, the subtle energy fields—the subtle bodies—of human beings are undergoing change as well, which is another factor creating stress in the outer world.

I've given much thought and inner research over the years into understand the nature of this new subtle body. I feel as though I've only scratched the surface. But it does seem to me that we are preparing for the incarnation of a new kind of humanity, perhaps preparing for our own future rebirths in service to the planet.

For now, I hope the exploration in this issue of the different dimensions of the Christ Event will provide you with fruitful reflection this Holiday Season when in many forms of celebration and belief, the Coming of Light and Love into the world is affirmed and welcomed. I feel it especially important to remember that the subtle worlds, knowing the sacredness birthing and arising in the depths of Gaia, resonate with joy.

I will let one of my subtle colleagues have the final word for this issue.

> Two thousand years ago, so legend has it, the angels sang, "Joy to the World." We would sing with you now a different song. We would sing to you, "Joy as the World" for Love arises within the Earth. Join us in being this Love. Join us in being this Joy.
> Blessings!

CHAPTER 5
Issue 28, June 2018

This issue is dedicated to completing the exploration into the idea of a "new subtle body" developing both for Gaia and for incarnating human beings.

The first indication I had of this was back in 1964, a year before I left college and began my current career as a "freelance mystic" and researcher of subtle realms. I had been asked to give the keynote address at a conference on "Youth and the New Age." At nineteen, I was the token youth, quite literally, as all the other attendees were in their late thirties, forties, and older. (I've written about this in my book, *Apprenticed to Spirit*.) As I got up to speak, I felt a powerful, loving presence enfold me and say, "Tell them that the 'New Age' is the manifestation of changes in the subtle realms of the Earth; a new planetary subtle body is emerging."

As a consequence, this image of a "new planetary subtle body" has been at the foundation of my work since the beginning. At nineteen and twenty years of age, I certainly could not claim to understand all that it meant; even now, over fifty years later, there is much I am still learning and still have to learn. To call this exploration a lifetime project is the simple truth.

Over the years, my subtle colleagues have often referred to the changes in Gaia's subtle body. Sometime in the late Seventies or early Eighties, as far as I can now remember, they also began broaching the topic of a similar change occurring in our own human subtle fields. Initially, this was simply a comment that it was happening without much explanation as to what this change entailed. Once I began researching and writing about our processes of incarnation and Incarnational Spirituality, I developed the tools and the concepts that I needed to investigate this idea with greater understanding.

Further, I was encouraged by the fact that a few other highly intuitive individuals whom I greatly respected and whose integrity, when it came to their own subtle contacts, I did not doubt, also began receiving communications about the emergence of "a new human subtle body." This let me know this was not an idea existing in my own mind alone.

Still, it was only in the past five years that I've begun to have deeper insights into just what this emergence was all about, aided by my contact with Mariel and later by a contact with an angelic presence involved with human evolution. This has brought this idea more and more into focus for me, and I've been feeling the time may be right to make it the subject of a more concerted research effort.

It has been my intent to make this subject of an emerging new subtle body a topic for *Views from the Borderland*. Before I start, though, I want to repeat what I always say: these field notes are one person's interpretation of subtle world contacts and experiences. You need to determine their worth and accuracy for you. This is very much a work in progress, and anything I write today is subject to change tomorrow if new and better information becomes available.

The Stick and the River

Imagine holding a large stick and thrusting it into a river so that it interrupts the flow of the current. When you do so, a vortex of swirling water forms around the stick. This eddy is made of the same material as the river, but it takes on its own identity as shaped by the contours of the stick itself. As long as the stick is in the water, the eddy will persist. Withdraw the stick, and the eddy disappears as it merges with the currents of the river.

The stick in the river provides us a useful metaphor for

understanding incarnation and the emergence of the subtle body. The stick represents the projection of the soul's presence into the Gaian energy fields of physical and subtle matter that make up the "river" of the Incarnate Realms. This projection is an energy-form in its own right, a "Body of Light" that holds and transmits the unique identity, intelligence, and intention of the soul that will form the core of the life-to-be. This Body of Light is resonant with love and with joy, two qualities needed to bring together and hold the substances that will develop into the physical and subtle bodies.

In particular, the soul's intent acts like the stick in the river. It forms a core, an energetic field, around which material from the subtle environment will gather and take shape as the subtle half of the emerging incarnate life. In Incarnational Spirituality, I call this energetic core of intention our Sovereignty. It attracts, holds, and organizes subtle matter into a unique subtle body, impressing it with our identity from the soul's own being.

What we call the "subtle environment" or the non-physical half of the Earth—and for that matter, most of the subtle worlds with which we are normally in contact, as well—are essentially Gaia's subtle body. The subtle matter that comprises these realms is part of Gaia. We could call it "Gaian matter" or "Gaian spirit."

Using the metaphor of the stick in the river, this means that our subtle bodies are both unique, individual expressions of ourselves and also comprised of material that is an emanation of Gaia's own being, just as the eddy is unique in its form but made up of the water flowing through the river. This is not at all unprecedented. Our physical bodies, though more solid than the energy form of the subtle body, are made up of cells that are both biologically part of the biosphere as a whole and individually identified and unique through our

DNA. In both our subtle and our physical makeup, we are structurally a singular identity and part of a larger whole at the same time. (And this isn't taking into account deeper levels of connection and interweaving that unfold from the Oneness behind and within all things.)

Being made of water, the eddy participates in the river as a whole even as it presents and manifests itself as a unique hydrodynamic phenomenon. Being made of Gaian subtle substance, our subtle body participates in the life and energy of Gaia as a whole, even as it manifests the unique identity of our incarnate self. The subtle body resonates with the subtle field of the Earth and vice versa.

This is important to realize. We think of our bodies, both physical and subtle, as *ours*, a private domain we alone inhabit. But we are constantly exchanging matter with our environment, taking material in and putting material out; in the process, we change and the environment changes. This is as true for the subtle body as for the physical one; the main difference is in the nature of what is exchanged. In this process, though, the boundaries between our bodies and our environment become indefinite. Physically, I could say my influence stops at the edge of my skin; chemically, though, this is not true. My influence, through pheromones, the carbon dioxide I breathe out, the waste material I excrete, and so on, is more far-reaching, and this is even more true of the energetic output and projections from the subtle body as a result of my thinking, feeling, willing and so on. Likewise, my environment influences me in a variety of ways on a variety of levels, from the food I take in to the thoughts and feelings I absorb from the world around me, to the subtle energies that I receive and incorporate from a wide variety of sources.

In biology, this mutual influence between organism and environment is called "coupling." Organisms are coupled with their environments. Change the latter, and the former need to adapt in some way or find a new environment. Change the organism, and it may change its environment in turn. This is as true for our subtle body as it is for our physical one.

For well over fifty years now, I have had indications from my inner colleagues that Gaia's planetary energy field is undergoing change and has been doing so for some time. The intuition felt by so many that a New Age is dawning or about to dawn is an inner recognition of these changes. A challenge is that this is not a single change but multiple layers of change, which can lead to differing perceptions of just when and how such a New Age may appear, what it will mean and what forms it might take. Nevertheless, I have thought of this change generally as a heightening of Gaia's life forces. To use the metaphor of Gaia as a river, I would say the change is a speeding up of its rate of flow, which provides more energy, more "force," with a consequence that much "silt" or polluted material has been stirred up in order to be washed away. Much of the turbulence we experience at the moment in human affairs seems to me to be a result of this stirring up.

When life is heightened, so is the impulse to manifest wholeness, which in turn increases the need for forming or deepening those connections and relationships on which that manifestation depends. For human beings, this means greater pressure for us to overcome our separations and express a more comprehensive and deeper level of interconnectedness and mutual support between ourselves and between us and the rest of the world. Developing and expressing the love and understanding necessary for this to happen is one of the major lessons confronting us: an inner "climate change" in order to deal with the outer one.

Our physical body locates us in space and establishes our identity and presence in the physical dimension of the world. Our subtle body similarly locates us in the subtle environment and provides the means for us to express ourselves in that dimension as well. Given the changes in the larger subtle field of the planet, it makes perfect sense that our subtle body will change as well to adapt. A heightening in the expression of connectedness and wholeness in the world will provide an impetus for the subtle body to heighten its own ability to form and hold the connections that enable it to be part of this energetically heightened environment.

For some years now, this is how I have thought about the "new subtle body." It represented an emergence of an expanded capacity for connectedness with the world around us. My question was "how?" How did this expansion take place? Was it through an alteration in the structure of the subtle body? Were new energies added to its constitution? Were new properties developed through adaptation? Was there an intervention of some nature by more highly developed beings, such as angels and Devas, connected to the evolution of Gaia? What caused—or was the nature of—the transition from the "current" subtle body to a new one? This remained unclear to me.

The Five Ps

One way I approached these questions was to explore the nature of the subtle body without worrying whether it's new or old. The subtle body may be understood as a set of interactive, interwoven functions, in much the same way that is true for our physical body with its various organs and "systems." While there are many subtle functions and activities one could identify, there are five that stand out for me. I think of them as the "Five P's." These are Participation,

Perception, Processing, Protection, and Projection.

Participation is the primary function. Incarnation is all about being present to and participating in the world we are in. Our physical body allows us to interact and engage with the physical world; the subtle body enables us to do the same with the subtle dimension of the world. Through this function, we are an active part of the subtle environment around us. The subtle body allows us to manifest our Presence, our soul's identity, on Earth as a subtle being as well as a physical one.

Perception is the ability of the subtle body to open and extend our awareness into the subtle environment. This function enables us to perceive and experience subtle energies, forces, and beings that may be present and active. It serves the same purpose in the non-physical side of our incarnation that our physical senses do for our physical life.

Processing is the "metabolic" function of the subtle body. It is the way it takes in subtle energies and qualities, assimilates them, integrates them, and makes them part of us. If, for instance, we receive a blessing of Light from a spiritual source, this is the function that receives that Light and makes it part of our life in a way we can use or benefit from, usually altering our own energy structure in some way to do so. In a way, it's the equivalent of the digestive and assimilative functions in our physical body.

Protection is a specific form of "processing" or subtle metabolism that is akin to the actions of the immune system in the physical body. This can take various forms depending on the need and the situation, from outright "hardening" of an energy boundary—that is to say, "shielding"—to absorbing and transmuting or transforming subtle forces that might otherwise be harmful to us.

Projection is the "broadcasting" or radiating function of

the subtle body, the means by which it influences and affects the subtle environment around it. It is a projection of subtle energies and qualities generated by us, mentally, emotionally, or spiritually. If I send blessings to another, I am utilizing this function. How the subtle body "broadcasts" and projects depends on the kind of subtle energy or quality we wish to radiate and on the nature of that to which the projection is directed. Sending a subtle energy to something specific, be it a person, an object or a place, is a different process from simply radiating a quality, such as calm or love, out into the environment (subtle and physical) as a whole.

Just as the physical body functions as a wholeness, even though we divide it up into "systems" such as the digestive system and the nervous system, the same is true for the subtle body. In one way, we can view it as a singular field of subtle energy shaped and held by our Sovereignty and Presence, that is to say, by the projection by the soul of its identity into the subtle dimension of the Earth.

Thus, the five functions I've described all work together and, in ways peculiar to the fluid nature of the subtle dimensions, blend together. Where it's easier to distinguish between the digestive system and the nervous system in the physical body because each is associated with distinct organs—for example, the stomach and the brain—in the subtle body, these functions are more diffused throughout the whole field itself.

Looking at the subtle body through the lens of these five functions, it seems to me the one most likely to change in the emergence of a new subtle body is Participation. Heightening the degree of connectedness or the power to connect in turn heightens the degree to which a new subtle body enables us to participate in the life of the world. An analogy might be living in a multi-lingual community. If I only speak one language, I can only interact meaningfully with others who share that language, which might be only a small proportion of the whole community population. However, the more languages I can speak and understand, the wider my sphere of connection and the greater my participation. It may well be that a new subtle body is master of a greater number of energetic "languages," allowing us to be more in tune with the physical and subtle life around us.

Likewise, it makes sense that our subtle sensitivity and perception may increase along with our ability to project blessing and energy into the world.

Useful as these Five Ps were in helping me visualize and understand the functions of the subtle body, my intuition said there is more to the emergence of a new subtle body than just a change in one or more of these functions. Looking at the subtle body in this way still didn't answer my basic questions.

An analogy would be comparing two models of cars together: one older, the other newer. Every year automobile manufacturers make changes in their models. Some of these changes are simply in appearance and styling; others might be to improve road handling or gas mileage. Such changes can make a welcome difference, but they don't really change the basic expression of the automobile. This year's model may burn fuel more efficiently than last year's, which is good, but it still has an internal combustion engine that uses fossil fuels. However, a change in the whole propulsion system, switching from a gasoline engine to an electric one, is significant. An electric car may look like a gas-powered car, but the impact it makes upon the environment is entirely different.

I felt that the way I was trying to understand the difference between the "old" and "new" subtle body was like looking at the difference between two different models of an internal combustion car. Yes, there were changes but it seemed to me that what I was sensing as the real change was actually something else, something that created a paradigm change, a larger picture or a different way of viewing things analogous to the switch from internal combustion to electric power. To grasp what I was missing, I needed to broaden my own thinking.

The Subtle Tool Box

To illustrate the direction my thinking went, here's a metaphor. Imagine that I'm building a house on my own. Every day I show up at the construction site with my toolbox. One day I'm putting the structure of the house together by creating the wooden framework. For this, I put carpentry tools into my toolbox. Then I decide to work on the plumbing. Now my toolbox has plumbing tools for me to use. Next, I want to install the electrical system. Now my toolbox has everything an electrician would need. Throughout the process, I'm working on manifesting the vision of the whole house but my toolbox contains what's needed for the particular part of that project on which I'm focused that day.

An important part of this metaphor is that the toolbox changes depending on what I need to accomplish in the moment; however the toolbox itselr is not experiencing evolutionary change. The carpenter's toolbox isn't evolving into the plumber's toolbox or the latter into the electrician's toolbox. The different toolboxes are connected to each other by the function of being a toolbox as well as by my intent and by the vision of the whole house, not by a developmental or evolutionary arc. That is, the nature of the toolbox at any given time is a function of my intention to work on a particular aspect of the house, guided by the vision of what the house needs in order to manifest. Further, whatever tools it contains, the toolbox represents that which I need in order to connect to and participate in the construction project. If the job of the day is to work on the electrical wiring, bringing a carpenter's toolbox will leave me disconnected from what is happening and unable to participate.

Thinking about an emerging new subtle body is really thinking about what kind of "toolbox" the construction work on Gaia's house needs right now and in the foreseeable future. What will allow us to connect with and participate in a world whose life energies are heightened and that seeks a greater manifestation of wholeness as a result?

The important part of this metaphor, though, and the part that helped me move past my own conceptual blockage, was this: the nature of the toolbox does not depend on the toolboxes that have gone before but on the intent of the contractor as he or she seeks to serve the vision of the house. The changing nature of the toolbox, that is, of the subtle body, is a function of the changing intent of the contractor, the soul. To understand the new subtle body, I need to understand the intent behind it.

This may not seem like much of a revelation, but for me, it was clarifying. Here's why.

Imagine that I'm studying the toolboxes that the contractor brings to the construction site. One day the toolbox is filled with things like hammers and nails, the next day with wrenches and pipe fittings, the third day with pliers and voltmeters and wire. How do I tell from this what will be in the toolbox on the fourth day? What will tomorrow's toolbox—the "emerging toolbox"—contain? If all I'm doing is studying the toolboxes, the best I can surmise is that the toolbox will continue to be a toolbox and will contain something useful; but I won't know from the toolboxes themselves specifically what that something may be.

To discover what will be in tomorrow's toolbox, I need

to see the vision of the whole house. What is needed next to bring the house into manifestation? Maybe I can even talk to the contractor to ask him or her what part of that vision is next in line to be worked upon and thus what tools he or she may need. What is his or her intent? I won't get the information I need from simply studying the toolboxes and the arrangement of contents within them (which, in a way, is what I have been doing).

Thinking about this prompted a comment from one of my subtle colleagues.

> Subtle Colleague: Yes, you've been overly focused on the structure and content of the subtle body. Changes are occurring there, yes, but then, subtle bodies are always undergoing change as the consciousnesses behind and within them develop and unfold. This is important, but it's not where you should be looking if you want to understand the deeper meaning and implications of the idea of a "new subtle body." Remember that not all human subtle bodies are the same, any more than individual bodies are the same. Physical bodies all obey certain biological principles and conform to the human genome, but within that framework, there are potentialities for near-infinite variation. The same is true at a subtle level. Whereas there are basic functions present in all subtle bodies, they are also influenced and shaped by the energy environments in which they develop and operate. These subtle environments can vary between places and cultures; the subtle energy field of India, for instance, is generally not the same as that in America. Would a "new subtle body" therefore be identical for all persons everywhere?
>
> What is important for you to look at here is not the structure of the subtle body but the intent that brings

that structure into being. The subtle body is intent made manifest. It is formed by the interaction of the soul's intent for the incarnation with the etheric and subtle substances of the incarnate dimension. The subtle body therefore holds the vision of the soul for that which the forthcoming embodiment is to achieve. On a physical level, this is equivalent to your personal genetic makeup: that which will shape and unfold your unique individuality.

However, the subtle body holds more than just the soul's intent. It holds as well the vision of what humanity may become. It holds the incarnational intent of the Oversoul of Humanity as a collective being. Physically, this would be metaphorically akin to the human genome: that which distinguishes you from other species of life.

Beyond that, the subtle body also holds and is shaped by the vision that Gaia holds for its life, of which humanity is a part. You might think of this as the structure of DNA itself, shared by all planetary life.

Thus, when you incarnate, your subtle body is formed by these three intents: that of your soul, that of Humanity, and that of Gaia. You carry within you seeds of individual, collective, and planetary vision that shape the destiny and potential of your incarnation. You may not fulfill any of them or only fulfill them partially, but they are there.

The intent of Gaia is constant in the timeframe of human evolution: to bring into being a planet rich with life and radiant with sacredness born of a wholeness co-created out of a diversity of consciousnesses, human and otherwise. To reflect this intent, there is that within your human subtle body that holds the power to connect and works to do so to bring wholeness into manifestation.

Within this constant, the intent of the Oversoul of Humanity is not always the same. It can vary from age to age as different aspects and qualities of human potential are emphasized or brought into play. Because of this, the human subtle body is not now the same as it was several millennia ago nor, even, several hundred years ago. In every age, it is shaped to best hold and manifest the vision of Humanity's Oversoul. For that matter, different parts of humanity may possess differently structured and differently enabled subtle bodies to correspond with whatever aspect of Humanity as a whole they are exploring and unfolding. The overriding intent, however, is to bring to the fore, eventually, a human consciousness able to actively and co-creatively support and implement the vision of Gaia. It is the vision of Humanity's identity as one of the formative forces of the world.

When the soul conceives the vision for a particular incarnation and shapes its intent -- its will -- accordingly, it does so, as much as it is able, in harmony with the vision of Gaia and with the vision of the Oversoul of Humanity that is active at that time. Within that context, however, it forms its own plan for the physical life to come and the expression of its individuality.

I should add that, once it is brought into being, there is a fourth force that is active in shaping the nature of the subtle body. This is the intent and actions of your incarnate agency, your personality or incarnate self. The choices you make, the decisions you make, the thoughts and feelings you entertain, all have an influence on the structure and shape of your subtle body just as they do on your physical body.

As you can see, examining the structure of the subtle body as a way of determining how it is evolving or what is emerging can be complex; in the end, it may not give you the information or understanding that you seek, in part because the future itself is still emerging. But you can simplify the process by looking past the structure to the intent. Perhaps the emergence you seek to understand is not that of the subtle body itself but an emergence of intent.

Thinking of the subtle body as a holder of vision and intent was very helpful and was a different way of looking at this issue for me. Going back to my metaphor, it's as if each toolbox, whatever its content may be that's appropriate to a specific task, carries with it a blueprint for the whole house. The specific tasks and thus the contents of the toolbox vary, but the blueprint basically remains constant. The toolboxes, however they may change, are the same in that they are always a means for implementing the blueprint. In large measure, they derive their meaning and importance from that blueprint and the way in which it defines the tasks that need to be accomplished.

Stepping Back

I want to step back a moment here and take a look at a larger picture. What has prompted this investigation for me? What have I been trying to achieve? Although I write about matters that most people would consider esoteric, those of you who have been following my work over the years know that I don't have that much interest in esoteric lore for its own sake. With all of the topics we discuss in this journal, my focus is mainly on how the material helps us in living our daily lives and in taking part in the collective life of Humanity and of Gaia. I am interested in understanding the subtle side of our world and of our lives in order to clarify how we can act and make a contribution. There is not one of us who is not in a position to make a difference, however small it may seem in the physical world. We are all generative souls and we carry that generativity into our incarnations.

The issue of an emerging new subtle body has, as I've mentioned, been on my mind for many years, always within the larger context of emerging changes in the subtle field and life of Gaia itself. I chose to focus on it in this year's issues of Views because I hoped that by doing so, it would bring new information to the fore but, more importantly, because I wanted to see if insights or tools would emerge that would be helpful to us in "Gaianeering," that is, consciously partnering with the unfolding life and purpose of Gaia in our changing world. The fact that a new subtle body is emerging is interesting, but what does this mean for us now? And is this emergence, as one of my friends wrote me, something we can affect and with which we can co-create or is it something that is happening to us as a consequence of evolution and thus something we discover after it happens?

Over the years as I've had discussion with people about this topic, the idea of a new subtle body has almost always led to speculation about new abilities and powers that this may bring to humanity. It's like asking, if our physical bodies are evolving, what will we be able to do in the future that we can't do now? If we develop a new subtle body, what will we be able to do that we can't do now?

I admit this is a fascinating question, and certainly, I have been fascinated by it. For a long time, this way of thinking about it has shaped my investigations. But taking this approach led me into a blind alley. Beyond a clear insight that we would gain an ability to be more connected to the rest of the world, better able to foster wholeness for ourselves and for Gaia, there was little further information, certainly none that I could use or easily articulate. And the insight of becoming better connected by itself is so general as to have little specific meaning. Of course we want to become better connected!

I want to be clear here that it's not that more detailed and precise information about the nature and structure of a new human subtle body is not available. All I'm saying is that it's not been available to *me*. At least not now. Perhaps it's more speculative than my particular subtle contacts wish to deal with. They are generally a results-oriented bunch. Given that the nature of any subtle body is interdependent with the environment in which it needs to function, it may simply be that the specific nature of humanity's subtle environment as the world goes through its changes is still unfolding, still indeterminate.

However, when the focus is switched to the intent that brings the subtle body into being, then possibilities emerge. To go back to my metaphor of the river, the stick, and the eddy, it's the stick that brings the eddy into being when we thrust it into the water. "The subtle body is intent made manifest," my subtle colleague said. "Perhaps the emergence you seek to understand is not that of the subtle body itself but an emergence of intent." In other words, perhaps we need to cast our attention to the stick and not place it so much upon the eddy. What intents are we embodying in our lives now? How are we holding the "stick?"

Angels and Sidhe

One of the complicating factors for me in thinking about a new emerging subtle body was a communication I had about three years ago from a source in the subtle worlds who was connected to this phenomenon. I didn't transcribe that particular contact at the time because I found this being's energy difficult to blend with because it was so different and so far removed from my own energy field. This created "static" for me that made me unsure about how accurately I was receiving and understanding his message. Also, language as I know and use it was not a familiar concept to him. I got the general drift of what he was communicating, but not enough that I felt confident reproducing it in words. However, I kept notes of my impressions.

It seemed to me he was saying that a new subtle body would contain elements of the Sidhe, bringing that side of our greater humanity to the fore and enabling it to be more a part of our own incarnational sensitivity. But he also said that we would be incorporating "angelic qualities." At least this was my impression, as the image I had was that of an angel merging with a human being. Whether he intended this, the result of his transmission in my imagination was an image of a subtle body that was part angel, part Sidhe, and part human.

I've thought about this particular encounter many times over the past years. It's one of those messages that seems dauntingly abstract, far removed from our everyday lives. It sounded like one of those weird experiments so beloved of science-fiction writers in which "angel DNA" and "Sidhe DNA" is mixed with human DNA to produce a new, hybrid being. Of course, this was taking the image too literally and concretely. On the other hand, I could not get clearer information as this contact did not come again. I think the being appreciated the challenge I had in connecting with it and holding its energy field.

Upon reflection, I realized that the image of the tri-partite subtle body was symbolic and not an actual description. One thing that stood out very clearly in that contact was that the idea of angelic and Sidhe qualities or energies had a very specific meaning to him. He was trying to portray a further step in the evolution of human beings to fully incarnate and embody our planetary identity as a formative force.

His reference to the Sidhe seemed to represent an

enhanced ability to appreciate and connect with the life within nature—perhaps related to the concept of *anwa* that my Sidhe contact Mariel has talked about and about which I've written in *Conversations with the Sidhe*. This is an ability that is innate within us but which is not well-represented or embodied in modern humanity.

As for the melding with angelic energies, this speaks to me again of an innate human quality to bless and to nurture the unfoldment of life, specifically the life of all the things and creatures in the world. For simplicity's sake, I think of Devas and nature spirits as cultivating and nurturing the forms of manifestation, whereas angels work with the unfoldment of the divinity within those forms, drawing out their sacred potentials, their sacred identities. Obviously, the line between these two functions—between "hardware" and "software," so to speak—is a very permeable membrane. The distinctions between angels and Devas, especially in the higher vibrational dimensions, are hard to see and may in fact be non-existent. But the image of "angel," which is what my visitor was tapping in my mind, refers in my thinking to the capacity to draw out the sacred within things; I'm sure, upon reflection, that this is what he was trying to convey.

In retrospect, what this being was showing me was essentially the same as information I'd had before: that the changes occurring in our subtle field are intended to enable us to better connect to the Earth. But by highlighting the images of the angelic and the Sidhe, he seemed to be trying to give me clues as to specific directions along which these changes were taking place.

I had not thought to bring up this communication, but while working on this issue, I had a conversation with the subtle colleague I call Philip, and he made reference to it. Here is what he said:

Philip: Greetings! What is occurring in the subtle dimensions of your world is an expansion both of potentiality and of expression. It's as if you were an organization and you received an influx of cash allowing you to expand your operations and undertake more activities than had been possible before. Some departments will remain the same, but other departments will need to change and broaden their outreach.

One change is in the incarnational process itself, allowing more elements of the soul and its Gaian connections to flow into the structure of the incarnation itself. It will mean an expanded subtle body, not necessarily in size but in complexity and capability. This is what the angelic contact you had some months ago was trying to say. Aspects of humanity that have been in reserve or have not had much scope for expression are now able to come forward and add themselves to the incarnational mix. The Sidhe are very much part of your larger human nature and capacity, and there are resonances that humanity has with the nature and function of the angelic kingdom. These capacities will be part of human incarnation in the future.

Think of it in a different way: as gaining a new, upgraded computer with much more processing power, more speed, more memory, and the capacity of running larger, more complex software.

The real change is not in your subtle body, which will continue to function as it always has. What is changing is in what might be called the incarnational "birth canal" through which the energies of the soul enter into connection with the physical world. Though physical metaphors do not accurately describe it, we could say that it is widening as part of the expansions taking place within Gaia's own being. A wider canal means a bigger baby can be born!

The innate capacity within each soul to manifest a Gaian consciousness has more "room" now in which to unfold and manifest in incarnation.

But this capacity is always there, and there is nothing preventing you from exercising your will and presence to expand yourself as you are now. Incarnation is a process, not an event, and is always happening within you, as you know. You can, through your intent and your attunement, widen your own immediate incarnational birth channel. Nothing prevents your own subtle body from expanding accordingly.

Remember: your subtle body—indeed, in a larger sense, your whole life—is vision incarnated.

Incarnating Vision

In exploring the idea of a new subtle body, I've spent a lot of time trying to determine its nature. To go back to my construction metaphor, it's like sitting and trying to imagine what new tools are going to be in the toolbox. This has not been all that fruitful. It has not been wasted effort, though, for I feel I've come out in a good place. That place is realizing that the answers lie in the blueprint—the vision. I pick the tools based on the job that needs doing, and that job is defined by the vision. If there are tools I need that I don't know how to acquire, I can have faith that they will come as I am doing the work. It has certainly manifested that way in my own life.

In my construction metaphor, the ultimate objective is to build a house. There may be different specific rooms and functions within that house, but the overall vision is the house. In Gaia's case, the "house" is planetary wholeness, the unobstructed flow of sacredness, love, and fulfillment through the entire web of interconnectedness that incorporates all that lives within the world (and that includes everything, even those things we see as inorganic). This is a big vision, but it translates into individual intent and action.

Can I intend, in the actions of my daily life, to foster, draw forth or create as much wholeness around me and within me as I can? Can this be my intention? Can I embody the vision of the wholeness of life and make that the cornerstone of my expression?

In my river and stick metaphor, that's how we wield the stick.

We have many sources helping us to discern and embody this vision: the spiritual wisdom of humanity, the Christ Event, the recent forthcoming of the Sidhe to add their wisdom and energy to our own, and many, many partners and allies in the subtle worlds. But when it comes down to it, only we can wield the stick of intent in our own lives. Only we can hold it in resonance and alignment with the vision of Gaia, becoming "Gaianeers."

There's much here still to be learned and explored, much still to uncover, but at this point in my own research, I am brought back to the importance and power of our individual choices. If the "incarnational birth canal" is widening to allow even more of the soul's being to come into embodiment, we can be, through our actions, part of that widening. Our love, our compassion, our care for each other, for the world, for ourselves, all contribute to this. We are, in a way, Gaia unfolding itself; at least, we are certainly part of that unfoldment, and we take part by consciously realizing that this is who we are and bringing that realization into what we are doing.

In this way, the story of a new subtle body isn't just some piece of abstract esoteric lore but the story of our own ongoing recreation of ourselves as incarnations of Gaia's vision, co-creators of a sacred world. Our subtle body is as alive with possibilities and capacities as we allow it to be through our thoughts, our feelings, and our actions. We don't have to imagine what a new subtle body may be like. It will emerge naturally as we imagine what connectedness looks like in our daily life and act to bring that imagination into a loving reality.

CHAPTER SIX
Issue 31, March, 2019

In this issue, we're going to explore an esoteric cosmology, guided by questions like "where did we come from," "who—or what—are we," "why are we here," "where are we going," and so forth. Obviously, our exploration won't be as extensive as an occult history by Helena Blavatsky, Rudolf Steiner, or Alice Bailey. There's only so much I can cram into a journal that averages 25 to 30 pages! I can, however, touch on a few highlights—milestones in our evolutionary journey as human beings.

In so doing, my approach is different from that taken by the authors I've mentioned and probably different from what most people would think of as an esoteric history or cosmology. For one thing, we live at the bottom of an incarnational "time well," just as we are at the bottom of Earth's gravity well. Here events and processes that seem "spherical" and multi-dimensional in the subtle worlds are flattened and compressed into chains of causation, giving us a sense of time as something linear, flowing from the past through the present and into the future.

Moving out of the Earth's gravity well enables a person to experience weightlessness and a domain in which there is no up or down, top or bottom, left or right (except as we name these things due to our own physical orientation). Similarly, as consciousness moves out of the "time well" of the incarnate realm, the phenomenon of time expands and becomes less and less compressed and constricted. Time doesn't cease to exist; it just becomes something very different from anything we experience here, more holistic and spatial than linear.

Trying to describe this state, we may call it "timeless" or say that everything is simultaneous, all happening at once, but I think neither of these descriptions is fully accurate. Words fail us. The simplest thing I can say is that as we move in consciousness out of our time well, past, present, and future don't cease to exist but take on different relationships to each other than the ones we're used to. They are joined by other dimensional elements for which we have no words or images to form a complex ecology of time and space in which simultaneity and linear causation are only two of many possible intertwining manifestations of beingness and presence.

This means that to speak of an esoteric, developmental, sequential "history" of consciousness or of the universe that proceeds from an originating point far back in the depths of time through countless millennia to the present day and beyond is not possible; it is essentially a narrative fiction born of the human need to create a straight road within an otherwise trackless wilderness of being. In a way, such an esoteric cosmology is an artifact of human thinking in the Nineteenth and Twentieth Centuries and is more a reflection of a way of seeing reality than they are a description of that reality itself.

But wait, someone may ask. What about the "Akashic Record" that adepts and sensitives are supposedly able to access? What about "cosmic memory?" Aren't all events and happenings recorded somewhere, imprinted on the Mind of God in much the way that past geological ages are revealed by the layers of rock strata? Isn't there a "Library" on the inner that tells the true history of human activity in the world? Is there no way to know about our past and where we have come from?

The deeper we are in the planetary time well, the more we do indeed find such records, libraries, memories, and imprints. But they are not always as definitive as we may expect, for the simple reason that what is recorded, generally speaking, are not *events* but *experiences*. This is not an unknown phenomenon. We all know how unreliable eyewitness testimony can be in a court of law. Two people can witness the same event but end up with different memories and descriptions of what happened because their experiences are different. I may go to Disneyland with my children and we all go on the same ride, but one child may laugh with pleasure and another may cry with fear. The ride-event is the same for each child, but the ride-memory is not. Which gets recorded in the "akashic record?" Both do. Which is the real description of the ride? Both are.

But, one may question, what about cameras and videos? Two eyewitnesses may see a crime being committed and tell two different stories, but a video of the event shows what really happens. Yes, this is true, although these days, even videos can be altered to show something different. Reality is becoming increasingly malleable through tools given us by the Internet and digital computing. But surely, the memory of God, the Akashic Record, the "Hall of Records of All Planetary Events" is like an uncorrupted, uncorruptible video camera, impersonally and flawlessly recording the history of the world? Isn't it?

Not in my experience (and again, I must emphasize that this is just *my* experience). The reason has nothing to do with whether the cosmic memory can be tampered with the way a computer hacker can tamper with a digitized video file. It has to do with what is remembered. Here is where our experience at the bottom of the time well flattens reality. Cameras only record the surface of things, but the cosmos remembers the interiority, the experience, the spirit of things, and this interiority is different for each life that is part of the experience.

What is "remembered" is much more complex than a simple event or chain of events.

For instance, I take a picture of all my family celebrating a birthday. Everyone is happy and smiling. Later, I can go back and look at that picture, and I see the smiling, happy faces. But what I don't see are the energy fields we were experiencing being together. I don't see the emotions that people were feeling behind the smiles. I don't see the thoughts in their minds. I may remember that my oldest son was tired that night after a long day of counseling teenagers or that my oldest daughter was stressed due to tensions at work, but none of that is in the picture. If I were to ask each of them what their memory of that party was, they would all say they had had a good time, but my son might say he was anxious for the party to end so he could go home and sleep, my daughter might say that behind her smile was worry about a work situation, my other son might be wishing we had a different flavor of ice cream, and so on. People are sharing happiness, but they are also inhabiting the experience of the party in their own unique ways.

What does the "cosmic memory," the "Akashic Record," or the "Inner Library" record? What does it say about that party? It presents a gestalt of all the experiences which, by the way, transcends psychological and physical aspects and includes what was happening in the subtle environment, with the techno-elemental life in the room where the party was taking place, and so on. And further, it doesn't "record" this as something happening in the "past" but as part of a larger "Now" that is the planetary presence.

To make things even more complex, it may record all or many of the possibilities present in the event. We could have had a different flavor of ice cream; my oldest son might not have been tired; my oldest daughter might have had a stress-free, happy day at work. Or all the events in their lives might have been the same but they reacted differently. My younger son chooses to enjoy the flavor of the ice cream; my oldest son throws off his sense of fatigue; my oldest daughter uses meditative skills to fill herself with calming energy that defuses the stress. All these possibilities may also be recorded for they are part of the larger wholeness of life in that moment.

If I go to "read" this record, my own consciousness and my own position in the time well can dictate what I perceive. It's the same phenomenon we experience when we read a book and then a year or two later, read the same book and discover things in it we hadn't seen the first time because our consciousness at the time wasn't able to do so. I may only be able to see certain information but not other information. The record may be complete but my perception and interpretation of it is not.

None of this means that there are not facts in the universe, only that our sense of what constitutes a fact here at the bottom of our time well, here in the particulate dimension of incarnation, may not the same as what the cosmos outside the confines of this well and dimension sees as facts. And to tell the esoteric history of humanity or of the cosmos, one has to understand and perceive the nature of facts as they exist outside the time well. This is exceedingly hard for an incarnate mind (well, for *my* incarnate mind, at least!), not only in the perception itself but in the translation of that perception into a language designed for the bottom of that well. The end result, as I said above, is as much (if not more) narrative and metaphor as it is objective truth, at least as we understand objectivity. It's the reason esoteric cosmologies often disagree with each other or paint very different pictures. Witnesses to the same event don't always agree!

Why am I doing this issue on an esoteric cosmology given

the challenges it presents? Well, two reasons. The first is that a number of subscribers asked me to do so, and the second is that I was interested in seeing if I could, in fact, do so. It was a challenge in that I would have to attune in consciousness to areas of the subtle realms that I normally don't visit or with which I have a connection, and meeting a challenge can be fun! Besides, all my work in Incarnational Spirituality is embedded in a cosmology that often goes unvoiced and simply assumed, at least by me. I thought it was time to bring it more up front.

In preparing for this journal, I've thought a lot on how to approach it. I basically spent a month contemplating various approaches, reaching out to various subtle beings whom I thought might help me, tuning into areas of the subtle worlds that I felt might have the information I was seeking. As I hope I've indicated above, it's not as simple as going down to the local library and opening a reference book—or Googling the information that I wanted to have.

For most of that month, nothing really worked. It was like trying to climb a rock face but with the wrong tools. I would make a contact, then it would slip away or I couldn't hold it. My usual subtle colleagues offered what they could, but they are not into cosmologies. It was like asking a group of biologists questions about quantum physics; it's just not their field of expertise.

Mostly what I needed, I realized, was a point of entry. The "field of information" labeled "Cosmology" was simply too vast. I couldn't find a way into it that I could hold onto. I needed way to orient myself, a "north star" or a guiding reference point that would give me access to some of the deeper realms of "cosmic" memory and provide "navigation" to help my mind make sense of what I might experience or perceive. This point of entry couldn't be anything abstract.

I tried that, and it wasn't working for me. Just tuning into "Cosmology" as a topic, like feeding the name into a digital search engine, wasn't grounded enough. To access and integrate the information I wanted, I needed a point of entry that was organic and anchored in the world around me.

I began to think wistfully of other, easier, topics I could write about for this journal!

Then, thinking back to some experiences I've had in the past, I realized I could be the point of entry. It wouldn't necessarily lead me into "cosmology" in the abstract but rather into the cosmological underpinnings of my own incarnation, which, being human, I felt would also be applicable to most everyone else. What links could I uncover in myself that would give me access, even in a limited way, to the deeper, "cosmological" memories or information that I was seeking? Perhaps the right question to ask wasn't "what is the cosmology 'out there?'" but "what is the cosmology 'in here,' within myself?"

With this thought, the path inward opened up in a way that I could navigate. The more I thought about it, the more sense it made, certainly in a biological way. After all, our bodies contain the cellular memory of millions of years of physical, biological evolution. We recapitulate this history as fetuses in our mothers' wombs. Our blood is chemically like the ancient oceans in which life first evolved. We embody and carry our physical history around with us as us. Might this not also be true of our spiritual history, our cosmological history? We may be at the bottom of a time well, but might we not carry an ecology of time within us that extends far beyond this well?

To formulate this idea in a way that I could use to organize this journal, I came up with this picture of a human cosmology within us that contains in relationship and interaction our sacred origins, our stellar sources, our connection to Gaia, the birth of the soul, and so on, right down to our incarnate life as a step in manifesting the Ideal Human and the Ideal Earth. Here's the picture:

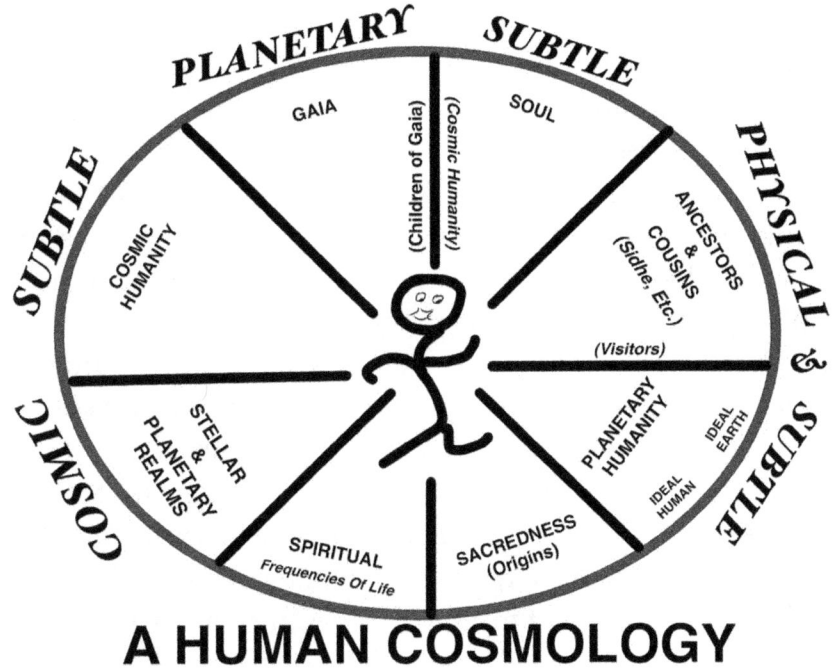

A HUMAN COSMOLOGY

For the rest of this journal, I'll use each of these categories to frame our exploration, beginning with our sacred origins and going clockwise around the circle to end with the Ideal Human and the Ideal Earth.

Sacredness (Origins)

Cosmologies often include origin stories: how did everything come into being? The cosmology of the physical universe postulates the Big Bang as the point of beginning. The physical universe, though, is only a part of a much larger *metaverse* that includes the subtle realms. Was there a "subtle

Big Bang" that brought the whole *metaverse* into existence?

I don't know. If so, it is beyond my powers of perception and awareness. No field notes based on personal experience are possible! It's why in recent years I have come to call the Sacred the "Generative Mystery." All creation, all time and space, all the multi-dimensions of the metaverse are generated by it, but how this happens is a mystery.

However, since I was a child, I have been aware of a Presence at the core of everything, permeating everything. This is not a being of any kind but more like a field of beingness which makes everything possible. I have felt how this Presence has no limit, expanding out into both the physical and subtle aspects of the universe.

This is a Presence that is well-known in the literature of mystical experience. Many people have sensed it and known it. In my own case, I have always had an inclination towards the mystical side of life and spirituality. Although for the past few years, my inner work has been engaged with the subtle realms, with subtle energies and beings such as I write about in this journal, most of my experiences growing up were of a mystical nature. Indeed, when I left college in 1965 to begin my spiritual work, I called myself a "freelance mystic."

Growing up, this Presence *was* the Sacred to me. I called it the Beloved because I experienced it as a presence of pure and all-embracing love. This is how I experience it today; for me, love is at the heart of the *metaverse*. At the same time, I recognize that calling the experience of this Presence as one of love is likely only my human way of perceiving it. It may be many other things as well, including qualities and potentialities of life which I cannot imagine or for which I have no names. However that may be, for me, this Presence is the Beloved of all creation.

In asking the cosmological questions of how it all began

or how did we begin, I felt my best chance to gain insights was to go into this Presence. Of all the mystical and subtle phenomena I've experienced in my life, it seems to me the most ancient, yet also the most timeless and the closest to the Source, if, in fact, it is not the Source itself.

When I attune to this Presence, what I experience is an infinite spaciousness and, as I have said, a quality of love. It is just me and this Presence and a oneness between us. Interestingly, this time, I found myself in the company of an actual being. This may only have been a projection into my consciousness of the Presence itself, taking a form with which I could relate as a person, or it may have been an actual angelic or Devic entity. I honestly do not know, and it doesn't really matter. The being didn't speak but gestured, and as it did so, it was like I began seeing a video or movie.

What I saw was the Presence spread out like a sea before me. I knew even as I observed this that what I was seeing was something tailored to my incarnated consciousness, giving a sense of time and space to what I was watching so that the scene would be meaningful in a way I could grasp. As I watched, I realized the sea of Presence was alive with activity. It was like seeing a supersaturated solution bursting with potentiality and life. Within the vastness of this Presence, points would emerge, setting the "sea" in motion like ripples around them. The words, "points of potentiation," came into my mind to describe what I was seeing. Some of these points appeared, then vanished; others lasted, their ripples joining with other ripples from other such points, coalescing into an even larger point of potentiation.

I felt that what I was seeing wasn't the emergence of beings or forces as such but rather the bubbling up from this Presence of potentiality: the potential for beings, energies, forces, qualities, and all the manifestations that make up the *metaverse.* Instead of a single "big bang," these "points of potentiation" constituted a multitude of starting points, each contributing in its way to the emergence of creation. Further, each of these points was a potentiation of the underlying Presence; there was no separation, only a difference of activity and focus.

I realized at the time and it is clear to me as I write this that this image is very similar to that of the quantum vacuum flux which, in quantum mechanics, is the ultimate substrate and process out of which the physical universe emerges. Subatomic particles, representing quantum relationships, emerge from this flux, some disappearing, others lasting and coalescing to form the protons, electrons, neutrons, quarks, and so on that make up the structure of atoms. While I do not equate the quantum vacuum flux with this primal Presence, there may well be correlates, the former reflecting in its activity the nature of the latter. Or it is just as likely that this is what I was shown because the idea of quantum vacuum flux is familiar to me and it was a convenient image with which to convey a suggestion of the Source and Origin of all that is. It doesn't really matter.

However, what *does* matter is that this process, however it may be described, isn't happening in time or space. Creation didn't happen eons ago in some galaxy far, far away. It is happening right now where we are. This creative process of "potentiation" (if I may call it that) is happening within us because the Presence of the Sacred is within us. There is a paradox here in that, certainly on a physical level, we are the products of a creative process, yet at the same time, we *are* that creative process. We are participating in it and with it.

This is not the same thing as saying we create our own reality or we are all gods or anything as concrete as that. These images from the New Age movement are incomplete and flawed when taken literally. But what is true is that we possesses generative capacities that make us partners in the ongoing unfoldment of the *metaverse*, and not only us but all life.

From our point of view, the Big Bang that was the origin of our physical universe was millions of years ago and far distant from us in space (for that matter, it created space as we know it). As I said earlier, here in the incarnate realms, we live at the bottom of a "time well," and this distorts the nature of what is happening outside that "well." The creative Presence is timelessly present and active, giving birth to creation right now all around us and within us, at the bottom of this "well" with us as well as in the infinite dimensions beyond.

We are not only products. We are collaborative, participatory sources.

Spiritual

The part of the cosmological story that I feel reasonably confident about, at least in its general outlines, begins with the appearance of what I call "Cosmic Humanity" and its eventual engagement with the Earth. But between that manifestation and the Presence that is the Source, there are other layers of beingness, filled with Intelligences and their activities. For simplicity's sake, I call these layers collectively the *Spiritual Realm*.

Here, "points of potency" in the creative Presence have coalesced into Intelligences that are Identities or beings. These Intelligences (for want of a better term) are neither gods nor goddesses, angels nor Devas but ultimately are the wombs from which gods, goddesses, angels, Devas, stars, and planets eventually emerge. They appear to my inner vision as vortices of life, concentrations of sacred potency, love, and will: purposeful whirlpools within the sea of Presence, an ocean of Light.

My sense of these Intelligences is that they are not ranked in any kind of hierarchy but are "entangled" together in a rich and complex network or ecology of beingness and creativity. One of these Intelligences could spawn an entire universe—perhaps our universe—while another could spawn something as small as an atom with all its intricate quantum complexity. Each would be equally demanding in a way, equally sacred, and neither Intelligence would be higher or lower, greater or lesser than the other.

I have no way of knowing the size or extent of the Spiritual Realm; it transcends measurement. Its role is to translate the potentials inherent in the activity within the Presence into actual manifestation and expression. Most of this manifestation is not at all physical. The physical universe we see, astoundingly vast as it is, is only a small part of the *metaverse*, most of which exists as the Spiritual Realm, as far as I can tell.

However, it does exist, as best I can put it, as a collection of frequencies of Life. These frequencies are differentiated by information. I've often used the metaphor of television broadcasts in trying to describe the interaction of the subtle realms with our physical world. My living room is filled with broadcasts from television networks such as ABC, NBC, PBS, Fox, CBS, BBC, and many others. They are all simultaneously present in the air around me; they are not layered one on top of another like a layer cake, nor are they segregated in space, with ABC over in one corner of the room and CBS in another. If my television set is broken and can only receive PBS broadcasts, all the others may as well not exist for me for I have no way of accessing the information they contain. Further, I know from experience that Fox will give me certain kinds of information while BBC will give me different information. If I want to experience the world of sports, I will tune into ESPN. If I want educational programming, I will watch PBS.

In short, all these networks embody different types of information and experience and they are co-equal; they are not in a hierarchical relationship to each other.

This is the best I can describe the different frequencies of life that make up the Spiritual Realm. They are proliferating, branching webs of distinct experience and potentiality, all ultimately set into motion and connected to one or more of the primal Intelligences that themselves are giving expression to the activity of potency within the sacred Presence. On all these webs, in all the universes and dimensions and inner planes unfolding from this activity, life in the form of distinct and varied beings, consciousnesses, and energies arise to embody, express, explore, and enhance the sacred information that that frequency carries.

Stellar And Planetary Realms

One of these primal spiritual "frequencies of life" is foundational to our universe and thus, ultimately, to our humanity and to you and me. From its creative potency arise the stellar and planetary realms. Initially, these exist only in the non-physical, subtle dimensions, in which what we think of in our world as "stars" and "planets" are the life-fields of great Beings and Intelligences. I think of these dimensions as the "Cosmic Subtle," as indicated in the drawing above.

In much esoteric literature, the cosmology of the inner worlds is marked by what I think of as *hierarchical emanationalism*. This simply means that a "higher realm" emanates or gives birth to a "lower realm," which in turn emanates a still lower realm or frequency. This creates the various "planes" that esotericists frequently write about.

In this scheme, the physical plane is at the bottom, more or less, the lowest dimension to be emanated and lesser in potency to the planes above it. By "rising up the planes," the esotericist is entering increasingly ever more spiritual and refined dimensions, rising closer and closer to the Godhead, the Source of all.

I do not doubt that the subtle dimensions can be experienced in this manner; many thousands of people have done so over the millennia. It is one way of mapping the territory, and it contains its share of truth. But the nature of the subtle planes is that they are notoriously difficult to map and describe because there can be a tendency for the map itself as a thought-form to shape what one experiences. If I expect to ascend through higher and higher planes of being, then chances are this is what I will experience; I will come to see the *metaverse* in which I live as something like a layer cake with God at the top and physical matter at the bottom.

The advantage I have here is that the primary elements of my cosmology were formed by experiences in childhood years before I encountered anything like an esoteric teaching. I didn't know what I should experience, so I had no expectations to shape my encounters with the subtle worlds. However, this doesn't mean that what I'm describing here or in my various books is the "correct truth." It's just that, in my ignorance of other ways of doing so, I was free to form my own maps of the inner worlds. Like any maps, they are incomplete. No map is the territory it describes, but different maps can give different perspectives, revealing insights that other ways of mapping and describing the territory may miss even while those other maps may give important insights of their own.

What stands out for me when I have explored the subtle realms is a joyful sense of artistry at work. Whether it's the cosmic subtle, the planetary subtle, or the subtle dimension of our own physical world, running throughout is a vibration of creativity, wonderment and discovery. It's as if the subtle worlds are crying out, "Hey, look what I can do! Isn't this amazing?" In the Christian tradition, there's an image of the angels of heaven ecstatically singing the praises of God, and in a way, this sense of awe, gratefulness, wonder, excitement, and love are signature elements of the subtle worlds I've experienced. Joy suffuses everything, a joy at being able to discover and unfold ever new potentials of life and being.

In this context, there are what I think of as "Environmentalists" on the one hand and "Explorers" and "Cultivators" on the other. The former create environments in which potentials can be discovered, revealed, and developed. In effect, new information can be generated: on a cosmic level, learning takes place. The latter enter into these environments to explore them and cultivate those potentials. They are learning what this environment has to offer and are growing in the process.

Another way to think of this is that the "Environmentalists" create spheres of opportunity within which the evolution of consciousness can take place or a particular set of potentials can be realized, and the "Explorers" are the ones who take advantage of these spheres. Both are generating new information, new insights, new ways of being within the *metaverse*.

Stars and planets are such "spheres of opportunity," environments created by one kind of consciousness in order to provide opportunities of life, growth, and exploration for other consciousnesses.

As I said, most of these stars and planets in the cosmic subtle dimensions have no physical nature; what differentiates them are the kind of environments they create for evolving consciousnesses and the manner in which they express the generativity of their innate sacredness. A being that is radiantly active in giving itself to empower others (a "star") may create an environment too intensely energetic for many emerging consciousnesses. The latter will go into life-spheres created by other beings ("planets") who can step down that radiance into a less intense form. The relationship between these types of beings is less hierarchical in my experience than it is collaborative, like a group of artists cooperating together and inspiring each other. And a being that is a "star" to some consciousnesses may itself be a "planet" to others, and vice versa.

I want to stress my experience here: while some Intelligences or beings are more experienced, skilled, powerful, and capable than others, this does not translate into ranks in which some beings are superior and others are inferior. The whole sense of ranking is a human projection. For beings who can directly experience the Presence of the sacred in each other, there can be no ranking for all are equal "in the eyes of God." Where hierarchy comes into play is in terms of function. A more experienced or powerful being may undertake a correspondingly more challenging and potent task. There is more involved in being the life-center or Soul of a solar system, for instance, than in being the life-center or Soul of a planet within that system. In this regard, hierarchies reflect function and responsibility, not the relative value of any being. Beings do not evolve to become "more sacred" but to become more equipped to express the potentials and responsibilities of their sacredness.

The physical universe can be seen as an environment for exploring potential, for discovery and creativity, for learning, and for growth, the same as any other environment. Indeed, where the cosmic subtle dimensions are concerned, the physical universe is simply another spiritual frequency or plane or environment, one among many. But it is an environment with certain restrictions and parameters that create a very different kind of experience for exploring consciousnesses than is normally found in the subtle worlds.

When the decision was made to bring the physical universe into being (and I do not know who or what made that decision; my supposition is that it was a collective decision on the part of a number of beings), beings capable of creating the new kinds of environments for physical life came forward to do so. Collectively, these beings make up what I think of as the "stellar realms."

Their incarnations as physical stars set the scene for other incarnations, such as those of planets and the beings that live upon them, to follow, giving rise over the millennia to the universe as we know it. As this evolution unfolded and the physical universe and its etheric counterpart became more complex and developed, beings who acted as planetary souls within the cosmic subtle realms began to guide planetary development in partnership with the solar beings. A subtle "planetary dimension" was brought into existence providing whole new environments for incarnation, exploration, and development.

Cosmic Humanity

Physical cosmologists tell us that we are all made of "star-stuff" since stars are the wombs that create and generate the atoms that are the building blocks of the physical universe. So, many millennia ago, the atoms in our bodies were formed in the nuclear fires at a star's heart.

That we come from stars is equally true on a subtle level. I have often written that there is a "Cosmic Humanity" and that it is this field of life and consciousness that seeded the Earth in cooperation with Gaia, ultimately giving rise to ourselves as a planetary humanity. How did this come about? What is this Cosmic Humanity?

Beings and forces from the stellar realms take many forms as they enter and interact with the physical universe and its subtle counterpart. The most obvious, of course, are the stars themselves. They may also manifest directly as planets, as I'll describe in a bit. In this case, though, what I was shown was a stellar being forming out of its own life and energy a field of activity that is, as best I can describe it, a "mobile star." That is, it has star-like functions of generativity, radiance, holopoiesis, and the power to nurture life and assist its development, but it is not located in a particular form or place. It can manifest where needed. It has a coherency of function and internal resonance, but it can express, much like a hive, though a multiplicity of beings. These beings are cosmic individualities, beings of Light and spirit, sparks uniting to form a common flame of service and Light. The result is a blend of a unified and unifying Spirit and many unique, differentiated spirits.

As I understand it, this stellar being had a function it wanted to perform in support of and in service to those of its colleagues and companions who were taking on the more fixed position of being a star or a planet. To attract spirits who wished to grow to embody and fulfill this function, thereby enhancing their own potential stellar nature, this being "sounded a note" (i.e. expressed and resonated an intention) which acted as something like a Want Ad: "Wanted: Spirits willing to develop skills of generativity, to undertake travel, and to offer service with no fixed location. Join up and see the Universe!"

Those who responded became Cosmic Humanity.

I've written elsewhere of my experience meeting a

snail-like being from another world while participating in a shamanic journey to a crossroads place within the subtle realms. As I've described, I felt a connection with this being and saw it as a fellow human even though in form we were very different. The reason was that I could discern the same "signature" of Cosmic Humanity in its field as I and all other terrestrial humans carry in our subtle fields. I could see that we came from the same stellar ancestor and were part of a common field of function.

The "Humanity" part of "Cosmic Humanity" doesn't refer to any particular form; there is nothing anthropocentric about it. Rather it refers to a set of spiritual and energetic functions that work to nurture the evolution of life in particular ways.

As I said, I see Cosmic Humanity—our ancestral Field of Being—as a form of "mobile star," an agent of stellar consciousness and life possessing a flexibility of expression and service that a "fixed star," like our sun, does not have. The function of this "mobile star" is to stimulate consciousnesses evolving within the environment of a planet in a way that awakens their innate presence of "star-ness," i.e. the generative, nurturing, life-empowering, and creative activity of the Sacred. This awakening allows these evolving planetary consciousnesses to resonate to and connect with the spiritual forces and potentials active within the stellar realms. There is more involved here, but this is, I confess, the best way I can describe it.

If I were to find a metaphor within our everyday human experience, Cosmic Humanity would be like the United Nations, an endeavor and presence made up of individuals from all the nations who have a planetary, trans-national perspective. People in the United Nations have language and cultural skills that enhance communication, collaboration, and cooperation between different people in order to foster wholeness in the world. Planets are like individual nations that have boundaries and within those boundaries, cultivate distinct national characteristics of language, culture, and society. The emphasis is on building the wholeness of the nation. But at some point, that nation wants to be a participant in the larger planetary whole. To enable this, teams of people from the United Nations come to that nation to live within its borders and to become citizens in order to form resonance and communal relationships with those who are native-born citizens. Out of this relationship, these UN representatives can awaken the national citizens to their planetary citizenship, helping them to see and connect to those who live beyond their boundaries.

This Cosmic Humanity or mobile star evolves through its interactions and engagements with solar systems and planets. The Field of Cosmic Humanity is a non-local phenomenon spread throughout the cosmos; whatever other functions it performs, it serves to assist the evolution of consciousness within planetary environments. Generally speaking, it localizes part of itself to merge with a particular planetary soul and its field, thereby creating a set of planetary souls that will in time incarnate in some manner upon that world. As these planetary souls evolve over millennia of planetary time, they gain new knowledge, experience, insights, wisdom, and capacities through interaction with planetary life. If they choose, they may then return to the Field of Cosmic Humanity, which becomes enriched by what they bring with them in their new states of beingness and life; the Field (and the stellar incarnation behind it) evolves accordingly and improves its ability to serve future generations of life throughout the universe. Individual members of this Field may also "graduate" and move on to undertake other functions, other services, other possibilities within the *metaverse*. In effect, those who were national citizens can enroll in the United Nations while those who have served the UN for awhile can leave to do other things.

It should be understood that the boundaries of this Field are dynamic and fluid. Beings come and go around the edges, dipping in to become part of Cosmic Humanity for a time and then leaving. As with so much of the subtle dimensions, boundaries are not so much limits as they are starting places for engagement, conversation, and negotiation.

Gaia

Cosmic Humanity is part of the cosmic subtle realms. With the creation of the Earth, there come into being what I think of as the *planetary subtle* dimensions, which are collectively the subtle body or life-field of Gaia, the Planetary Soul, as it manifests within our universe. When I usually write about the subtle worlds, it is this collection of planetary subtle frequencies or "planes" to which I am referring. The subtle environment, however, is different. This is the etheric or immediate subtle correspondence to the physical world. (In my book, *Subtle Worlds*, I use the relationship of ocean and land to illustrate these differences: the deep ocean is the cosmic subtle, the ocean over the continental shelf is the planetary subtle, and the sea shore with its tidal pools and shallows, where land and sea intermingle, is the subtle environment—which includes the *etheric* dimension—with the land metaphorically being the physical world.)

Mariel is a Sidhe woman who is my principal contact with these "cousins" of incarnate humanity. I have chronicled my evolving relationship and work with her in my books *Conversations with the Sidhe* and *Engaging the Sidhe*, as well as in the *Card Deck of the Sidhe*. In a communication with me, she said that Gaia, the soul of our world, is the incarnation of a stellar being who wished to be a "star of life" instead of a star of energy such as our sun.

I do not know if such a stellar incarnation is a common or uncommon occurrence. There are distinctions here that are challenging to put into words. But let me see what I can tease out of the web of impressions that come when I attune to this.

Stellar and planetary realms are not different from each other in terms of sacredness. One is not more sacred or "closer to God" than the other. And in the non-physical side of the *metaverse,* stars and planets are not balls of nuclear fire or balls of solid matter. They are fields, energetic environments within which life and consciousness can evolve, explore, and perform particular functions. The main difference is that those beings who become the Souls of planets are creating specialized fields in which certain kinds of exploration and experimentation can take place or certain kinds of "soul skill sets" can be developed. A "planet," whether in subtle or physical form, provides a more focused environment than do those beings who are the souls of stars.

In this sense, I think of "planets" as a combination of nursery and trade school. They are places in which new "units of consciousness" can be born and developed, and they are places where specific skills can be learned. The Planetary Souls generally provide a less intense energetic environment than do the Stellar Beings.

To the best of my understanding, what differentiates the consciousness of a being that has evolved within a planetary environment and one who has evolved and functions within the stellar realms is a capacity for generativity and connectedness. The difference is one of vibration and something I might call "vividness." It's hard to name because there's nothing in our physical world that exactly compares to it. A stellar being might seem to be in human terms more radiant and more engaged in the life of the cosmos. It is energetically more expressive, and to us, this might seem as if it is more capable of loving "universally." Maybe, using modern computer language, an analogy might be to say that stellar consciousness has greater "bandwidth" than does planetary consciousness and thus is an instrument for a greater flow of information and capacity. These are simple markers of difference which I admit may not be all that accurate but which can be useful in our discussion here. And it needs to be kept in mind that in order to achieve certain ends, the conditions of a planet may be such as to deliberately restrict or lesson that bandwidth. This is certainly true when we consider the nature of life and consciousness within the physical vibration of matter as we know it.

Now imagine that a particular stellar being wished to translate its radiant, generative energy—its "star-ness"—into becoming a "star of life" within the physical universe. This means two things. First, that its life-field would support a rich and diverse ecology of physical life. Second, that in so doing, it would become a "trade school" for developing forms of physical life in which the stellar consciousness was awakened and embodied as an internal presence rather than as an external radiance. In effect, the qualities and nature of the stellar realms would become incarnated within the physical universe.

This is what Mariel is implying when she says that Gaia is the incarnation of a stellar being. She does not say it is the only stellar being doing this in the universe; I have no idea if she knows how common or rare a phenomenon this is. But rare or not, it affects the course of consciousness evolution on this planet. For one thing, to accomplish this goal of nurturing the evolution of consciousnesses that could embody qualities from the stellar realms, Gaia sought assistance.

Help came in the form of a "mobile star," Cosmic Humanity. Within this Field (which, I remind you, is non-local in its nature; it's not like a cloud floating through space from planet to planet), those individual spirits who wished to become part of the Gaian experiment did so. They brought with them their attunement to stellar realms and, in many cases, experiences gained from previous incarnations and "terms of service" in other planetary systems. In the merging of these elements of Cosmic Humanity with Gaia, what we know as the human soul came into being.

SOUL

The term "soul" is used in a variety of contexts in esoterics, spirituality, religion, and culture, and each context gives it a different meaning. So, I want to be clear here what I am describing. What I mean by "the soul" is an instrument for engaging with the life-field and intentions of Gaia and a vehicle for the evolution of a mode of consciousness that results from that engagement. The human soul became the template, the "seed," for the development and embodiment of a stellar form of Gaian consciousness and a Gaian form of stellar consciousness. It was a matrix for the qualities of the stellar realm to incarnate within the realm of physical matter.

I've often referred to the soul as a highly complex field of consciousness, and the picture below explains why.

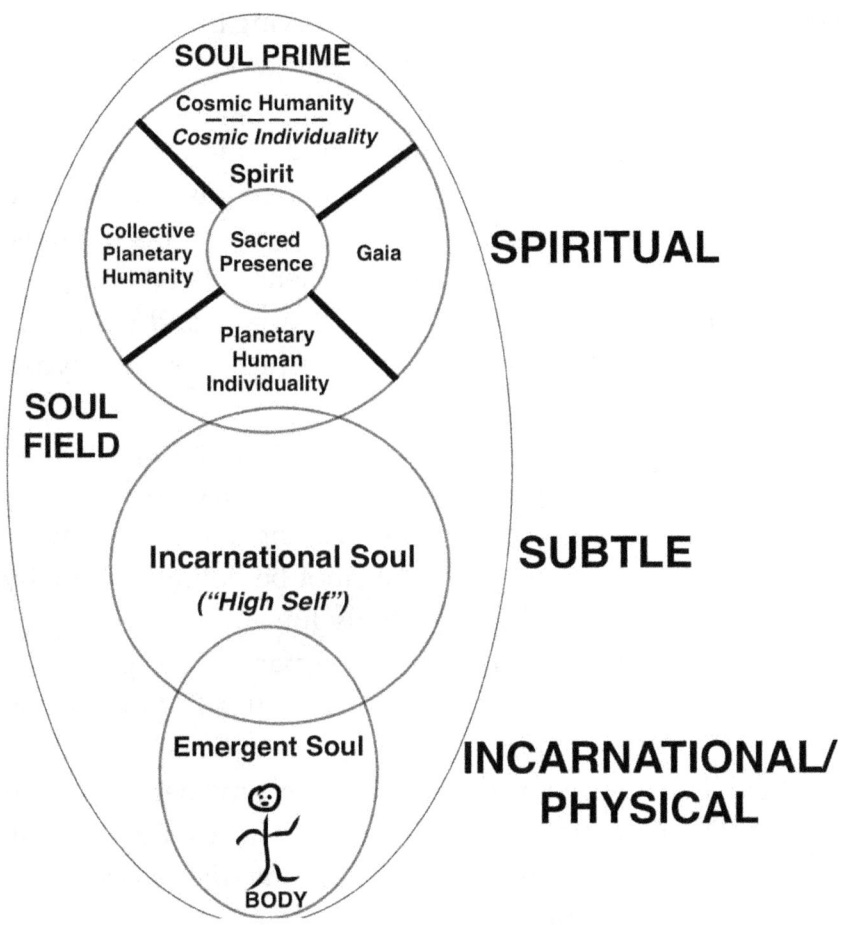

I think of the soul as a whole field which, when we are in incarnation, consists of three elements. There is "Soul Prime," the soul born from the merging of Cosmic Humanity with Gaia. This aspect of soul exists in the spiritual or soul realms of Gaia. As the picture shows, part of Soul Prime is aware of and engaged with the Field of Cosmic Humanity and its stellar origins; it is attuned to and nourished by its spirit or cosmic individuality.

Part of the soul's consciousness and energy is engaged with the World Soul, Gaia; part of it is engaged with the collective energy field of humanity evolving in the subtle and physical dimensions of this world; and part of it is involved with all that is required for the development of its unique planetary human individuality: its cosmic individuality reflected in the frequencies of matter. It is this part, I think, that many people associate with their soul for it is the most recognizably human and personal element. The other aspects of soul are "trans-human" for the most part and operating in ways that have little direct relationship to our everyday human world.

It is the fact that the Soul Prime is aware of and involved with all these four aspects (and perhaps others as well) that always gives me the impression of it being a complex, multi-dimensional field of being that cannot be defined solely by the characteristics of a single earthly life.

When we take incarnation, some part of the planetary human aspect of Soul Prime dedicates itself, its attention and its energy, to that incarnation as a holistic event, not yet "flattened" by a time well into the linear time between birth and death. This becomes what I call the Incarnational Soul, called by some the "High Self." For many, *this* is what they recognize as the soul.

Once incarnation takes place and the physical personality is developing, a new aspect of soul comes to the fore, which I call the Emergent Soul. This is the soul within us that operates in time and space as we know them, configuring itself to the specific conditions of our physical incarnation. It's the part of our soul that is learning and growing through direct engagement with physical life. The importance of recognizing this aspect of soul is that it keeps soul from being entirely something "out there," distant from our lives, and restores it to being "in here" as our Sovereignty, Self-Light, and Presence.

What is important is to realize that these three aspects of soul are just that, aspects. All of them together are the "whole soul" when we are in incarnation.

One final thing to point out. At the center of Soul Prime (and thus of the soul field as a whole) is "Sacred Presence." This is just what it says: the Source Presence of creation active within us, as I described earlier. Think of this inner Presence as the "Sovereignty of Creation;" just as our Sovereignty is a link between soul and the incarnate self, so this inner space of sacredness and Presence in us is the Sovereignty that links our soul, our Identity, our Spirit, to the Generative Mystery, to the Beloved.

In the beginning of its earthly engagement, this soul is more active in its stellar or Cosmic Humanity dimension. It may be an "old soul" in cosmic terms but a young, newborn soul in its Gaian context. It has to learn how to adjust to Gaia's field of life. There is no collective planetary humanity yet, and it has not yet developed a planetary human self because its incarnational forms have yet to evolve. All of this development will take time. Millennia may pass before the first truly human individuals begin to appear as incarnations in the physical world, millennia during which the soul is increasingly active in the subtle dimensions of Gaia and thereby increasingly taking on a Gaian "vibe" and consciousness, rounding out the other three quadrants in the Soul Prime picture above.

Ancestors And Cousins

What I've described above sounds very straight-forward, and I've deliberately written it as such to have a clear narrative of relationships and events. But in fact, the emergence of humanity in this world is far more complex and involves the convergence of multiple lines of evolution.

Because of limitations of space and, frankly, limits to my own perceptual abilities, I am having to tell this story in a focused, abbreviated way, hitting, as I said at the beginning, the high points as I am able to discern them. My guiding question has been, "Where do we as modern humanity come from?" What is our evolutionary story from an inner standpoint? For this reason, I've concentrated my narrative on Cosmic Humanity as it's our most direct subtle antecedent (if something happening millions of years ago in physical time can be considered "direct").

The challenge to this narrative, though, is that its focus can give rise to a sense of "human exceptionalism," as if we are the only species destined to embody stellar energies and consciousness. Our species already sees itself as privileged and as being at the summit of evolution, though recent events are calling this into question. From the point of view of the subtle worlds—and I am very confident of this perception—we do have a service to perform that is uniquely within our purview but we are far from being the most highly developed form of consciousness in our world nor the only one able to connect to and work with cosmic sources and stellar energies.

The fact is that just as Cosmic Humanity came to help Gaia with its objectives, so did other cosmic entities. Other stellar beings, the solar Angel of our system, other planetary souls, and their emissaries, have all pitched in over the millennia in one way or another. Some have sponsored and overlighted other species than our own. Some, such as many of the nature spirits and the beings of Faerie, have evolved out of Gaia itself, partaking of its stellar and planetary energetic characteristics.

As I understand it, the intersection of Gaia and the Field of Cosmic Humanity did not happen until the process of planetary evolution was already far along, and when it did occur, it was not a single event but a series of events, like successive waves. Each wave brought certain qualities, certain energies, certain capacities into the planetary sphere, leaving its mark and then withdrawing. Subsequent waves would build on what had been deposited in consciousness and energy, carrying the impulse of what has become human consciousness deeper into planetary involvement and development. And to these waves, other sources added their contributions, not least of which were the complementary waves of development arising out of Gaia. Indeed, it was the latter that set the pace and rhythm, providing progressive fields of consciousness and form with which the energies of stellar humanity could merge and blend.

What I have been shown of this process is that the early "waves" of life, energy, and consciousness emanating from Cosmic Humanity enveloped the evolving life upon the earth like a mist, exploring connections and possibilities. It intermingled with other evolutionary streams, such as those of plants and animals within nature. As I understand it, it was not clear at the outset just what form or combinations of forms would best serve to embody and give optimal expression to the gifts and potentials brought by Cosmic Humanity. Furthermore, to perform its function, the collective field of Planetary Humanity needed to be attuned to all the forms of life on earth; it needed to embody Gaia as well as Cosmic Humanity.

As a consequence, there were forms of humanity that appeared (mostly in the subtle worlds but in some cases in the physical) that we probably would not recognize now as "human" (certainly not as hominids) and then were allowed to die out either when they proved unsuitable or when their function of attunement had been fulfilled.

The evolutionary line of modern humanity contains the beings I have been calling the Sidhe as our most recent kin, but trace the line back further as it extends through the subtle realms of Gaia and, like a river spreading out into a delta, it broadens into a diversity of experiments and embodiments, successes and failures. Once Mariel made a humorous comment to me about what humanity was like in the far distant past when we were experimenting being "plant people." My mind immediately went to images of Groot, the sentient plant humanoid in the *Guardian of the Galaxy* movies (though, I realize, I could have easily thought of the Ents from Tolkein's *Lord of the Rings*.) Eventually, the primate humanoid form won out as most suitable, becoming the form through which we define humanity. Still, many of the legendary human-animal and human-plant hybrids we find in the mythologies of ancient cultures, creatures half-human and half-something else, may come from a deep species memory of those very ancient experiments of incarnation within the other kingdoms of nature.

The key point is that to do its job, planetary humanity needed to be intimately blended with the rest of planetary life. Everything on earth contains within itself the diffused frequency of Cosmic Humanity and all humans contain diffused within themselves the vibrations of all other Gaian life. Thus, we have had many "ancestors" and a host of "cousins," such as the Sidhe, who have contributed to the evolution of humanity or have had parallel evolutions alongside, all in service to Gaia's ultimate objectives to radiate sacred life out into the incarnate cosmos. Some of these ancestors and cousins long ago passed on back into the stellar and cosmic realms or are assisting with other planetary evolutions. Others are still present in the subtle realms, helping as and when they can. And some, like the Sidhe, after a time of separation, seem to be coming back into closer contact and cooperation in order to assist humanity in taking a further step towards its stellar heritage.

Planetary Humanity

In the physical fossil record of human life on earth, we can trace the rise of *Homo Sapiens* and the decline and disappearance of other branches of the human family, such as *Homo Neanderthalis*. As I've just written, there is a "fossil" record in the subtle worlds, too. There we can see that other manifestations of the Cosmic Humanity impulse didn't continue. There is no guarantee that we will continue, either. We may end up being yet another failed experiment, requiring a whole different form of Cosmic Humanity to appear on the planet. But at the moment, in spite of troubling world events, the "Gaian wind" is at our backs. I see no indication in the subtle worlds that our version of humanity has run its course and is about to expire.

Nevertheless, modern planetary humanity is under great pressure to breakthrough into a Gaian awareness and a recognition of its sacred past and future. Our heritage as both stellar and planetary humans pushes to be expressed. We seek to reclaim our power to create individual, collective, and planetary wholeness.

Within each of us is a memory of the vision of humanity, not as a particular form but as a holistic, generative, loving state of consciousness: the ideal human. Likewise, within each of us is a knowledge of what Gaia seeks to become, in part through our efforts and awareness: the image of the ideal earth. These two are like twin pillars at the entrance to our inner temple or sacred space, the place where we can touch the ever-present Presence of the Beloved, the source Presence of creation.

This was emphasized for me in a vision I had many years ago. I found myself standing in front of a small temple-like building, a simple structure with a domed roof. The doorway was flanked by two pillars. I knew instinctively that one represented the life, the love, the passion, the imagination, the will, the creativity, the potentials that went into the formation of Cosmic Humanity out of the life of one or more stellar beings. Although it took the form of a pillar, I knew there was nothing static about this presence. It held both the dynamic, sacred idea that gave birth to Cosmic Humanity and the vision of the Gaian humanity that is emerging on this planet as a union of planetary and stellar energies. I called this the Pillar of the Ideal Human.

The other pillar was similar except that it represented the life, love, passion, will, imagination, creativity that went into the formation of Gaia by its stellar forbears. It, too, was a seed out of which this world in all its ages and all its manifestation has been unfolding. I called this the Pillar of the Ideal Earth.

The temple enclosed and thus highlighted an inner, sacred space, a place of creative Presence and Silence. This space is where our individuality and our sacredness, our humanity and nature, the stellar and the planetary converge and release a Light of wholeness, a Light that renews and blesses all that it encounters. This is the Light of our sacredness but also the Light of our cosmic and our planetary humanity becoming one. It is the emergent Light of our incarnation as part of Gaia.

In my recent classes, I've been offering the following exercise as a way of visualizing and attuning to this Light, drawing on the support of the "Ideal Human" and the "Ideal Earth." I call it the "Temple Exercise."

THE TEMPLE EXERCISE

Picture a sacred space. I call it the inner Temple, but it can take any shape and need not be a building at all. However, there is one requirement: entry into this Temple or sacred space is by passing between two pillars or trees (or two distinct sides of an opening). One of these represents the Ideal Human, the other the Ideal Earth.

These «Ideal» pillars do not represent specific states or objectives but rather represent the dynamic energies involved in drawing forth the sacred potentials inherent in humanity and the Earth. How these potentials may manifest in form is not as important as touching into the presence and felt sense of these «impulses of unfoldment.»

Within the Temple is our Incarnate Light, our Incarnate and Emergent Soul, our incarnational sacredness. We enter this space just as we enter incarnation, by aligning with the energies of the Ideal Human and the Ideal Earth. Each of these pillars and their impulses of unfoldment are part of each of us. In effect, we enter incarnation by pledging to serve and to embody the willingness and energy to bring forth to whatever degree we can the spirit of the Ideal Human and the spirit of the Ideal Earth. Our souls commit to contributing something, however little, however large, to the emergence of these potentials and their convergence in a state of wholeness. Ultimately, they are symbols of our own potentials, our own emergence, and our own wholeness.

This exercise can be done entirely in your imagination through visualization. If you wish to do this as an externalized ritual, which can be powerful in its own way, then you will need three candles of them. Ideally, they would be of three different colors, one for the Ideal Human, one for the Ideal Earth, and one for your incarnation, the Sovereignty, Self-Light, and presence you bring into your everyday affairs as your gifts to the world.

EXERCISE:

Visualize your inner Temple. The entryway is flanked by two pillars, the Spirit of the Ideal Human and the Spirit of the Ideal Earth. *(If you are using candles, light one candle for the Ideal Human and one candle for the Ideal Earth. Set them physically apart as if they are pillars on either side of an entrance. In your mind›s eye, visualize them as such, as Pillars of Light embodying the presence, energy, and spirit of the Ideal Human and the Ideal Earth.)*

Take a moment to attune to what each of these Pillars represents and feels like to you. What is their felt sense within you, within your body, within your whole being?

Now visualize yourself stepping past these Pillars into the inner Sanctuary of the Temple itself, whatever this may look like or feel like to you. In this place, there is only Light: the Light at the Origin of All Things, the Light that Renews, the Light of your Soul, the Light of Sacredness within you.

Take as long as you wish just to be with this Light in this sacred space. What does this feel like? What is its felt sense within you, within your body, within your whole being?

Fill yourself with this Light. Let it fill all parts of you in wholeness. Let it fill your Sovereignty. Let it fill your Self-Light. What does this feel like?

When you are ready, step back through the twin Pillars of the Ideal Human and the Ideal Earth. You are carrying this Light within you--and *as* you--as you enter your incarnation, your daily life as an embodied person. *(If you are using physical candles, light the third candle, representing your everyday incarnate self. This flame is your incarnational Light.)*

As you stand, back in your everyday environment, *(and as you light the third candle if you are using one)*, give thanks for this Light within you and within the world, the Light that Renews, the Light that Blesses, the Light that calls forth the Ideal Human and the Ideal Earth in loving relationship with each other. Make a statement of willing commitment to embody this Light in your life and offer it as a gift to the world, using whatever words, feelings, and images are meaningful to you.

Take a moment of silence to feel the incarnational Light and the spirits of the Ideal Human and the Ideal Earth within you, *as* you.

(*Blow out all the candles if you are using them.*) Take a moment to stand in your Sovereignty, honoring yourself as a bearer of Light. Then go about your daily affairs.

The nice thing is that once you have a felt sense of this Temple and of its Light, you can enter it through the two pillars anytime you wish during the day. It is always there within you and as part of you.

A Cosmological Journey

Here in the incarnate realm at the bottom of a time well, we experience the flow from past to future. We experience *journey*. Looked at from this perspective, the cosmology we've explored ever so briefly could look like this as we move from Presence into a potentially cosmic future fulfilling the promises inherent in the spirit of the Ideal Human and the Ideal Earth.

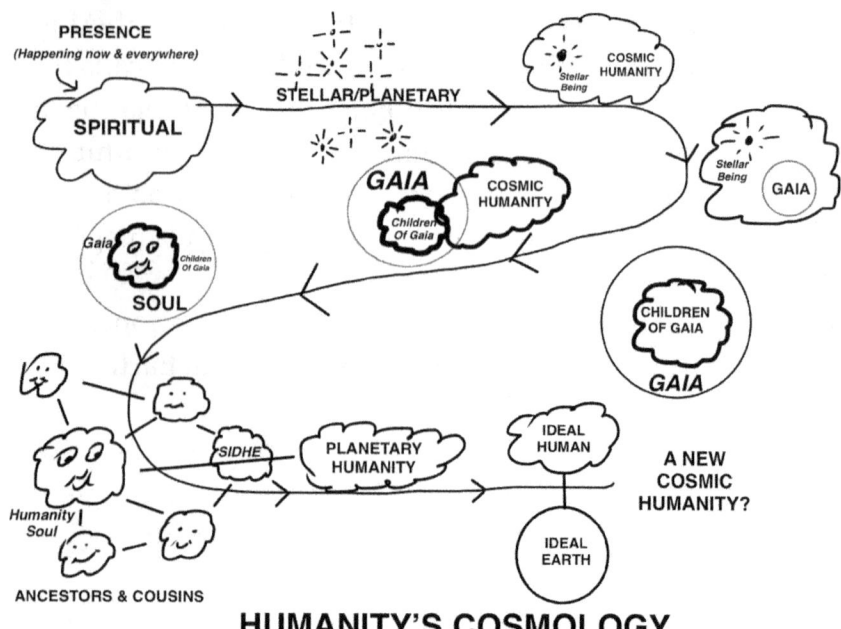

HUMANITY'S COSMOLOGY

This may be a useful way to look at it, but at the same time, for me, the key insight of this exploration into cosmology and thus of this issue of *Views*, is that we are not so much the products of a cosmological process as we contain the whole of it within us. We are embodied cosmology, incarnate cosmology. What we think of as the "past" is still present and active within us, constantly being shaped by our actions and our states of being. Our cosmology is really an ecology of consciousness, connection, and potential always active within us.

As I said, in this issue, I've necessarily focused on the human journey. Other species that share this world with us and other beings in the subtle realms as well have their own, equally important, equally sacred cosmologies. There could be, for instance, the Ideal Tree and the Ideal Earth, or the Ideal Dolphin and the Ideal Earth, or, as with the being whom I met in my inner journey, the Ideal "Snail" and the Ideal

Earth. We are special only insofar as we learn to serve with greater awareness and skill the ever-emerging wholeness of the Sacred.

And yet, through our cosmological journey, we have learned how our humanity includes all these others. This is treasured knowledge but also buried knowledge in our culture, something yet to surface in an outpouring of appreciation and love for all our kin who share this world with us. Perhaps that time is close at hand. I hope so. When that time comes—and in one way or another, I know it will—we will take a giant step forward to manifesting a Gaian humanity as a demonstration of what Cosmic Humanity is all about.

APPENDIX
THE GRAIL SPACE EXERCISE

I use the term "Grail Space" to mean any space that holds sacredness, just as in legend the Holy Grail held the transformative and renewing blood of Christ. Sacredness in this instance manifests as the incarnational consciousness and process that brings creation into being and sustains it in its unfoldment

We live in Grail Space. The entire cosmos is the primal Grail Space holding the sacredness of the Generative Mystery which I call the Sacred. But this primal Grail Space can be accentuated in local space at any time that we invoke the presence and flow of sacredness by honoring the incarnational process through which it manifests.

The practice of creating a local Grail space is one of standing in our own Sovereignty and Self-Light and engaging the local environment around us to evoke more fully the Life and Light that flows from the primal Grail Space, i.e. from the Sacred itself. Fundamentally, this is a practice of connecting through Presence and love with everything around us. It is an act of honoring and relating to our environment, inviting the life within it to respond energetically and express its own Grail capacities. It is the act of mutual holding that turns the environment, with ourselves in it, into a Grail in which sacredness may shine forth.

This may also be seen as affirming an "environmental Presence." That is, just as the Presence exercise attunes to and affirms a sacred, generative, holopoietic Presence within us at the heart of our incarnation, so Grail Space is attuning to and affirming such a Presence within the local surrounding environment of which we are a part.

The creation of Grail Space is a reciprocal act, not something we do to anything else. It is an act of extending an invitation, allowing the environment to respond as fully as it can in the moment. Grail Space is born of relationship and mutual engagement based on honoring the sovereignty and identity of all involved.

Creating Grail Space is really a simple process, but I break it down into a number of steps just so you can get a sense of the procedure. To read it, it can seem like a lot, but it's really a very fast, simple process. The main difference between this technique and simply sending love into your environment is the act of honoring and connecting with the identity of everything about you in a partnership. It is not you doing something to the things in your environment. It is you joining with them in collaboration to create a mutually beneficial space or field into which sacredness may be invoked.

One way to think of this is as if everything in your environment is alive and a person and you are joining hands with them to form a great circle. This circle creates the Grail Space, and into it sacredness is invoked.

THE EXERCISE

Begin by standing in your own Sovereignty, in the felt sense of your unique identity and your connection to your soul and to the sacred. If you wish, you can imagine this Sovereignty as a "spine" of Light within you, an axis around which your physical and subtle bodies develop and align.

Imagine this spine of Light becoming brighter and brighter as it unfolds from the love within your Soul and within the Sacred of which it is a part. As this Light becomes brighter within you, it expands and enfolds you.

Imagine yourself standing in an oval of Light emanating from your "spine" of Sovereignty and individuality, an oval that surrounds you on all sides, top and bottom, connecting you with the energies of the world. It forms and radiates from you as a personal Grail, an incarnational field holding sacredness.

Everything in your immediate environment is an expression of the Sacred. Everything you see participates in the primal Grail Space. Everything has within itself a "spine" of incarnational intent and Light, its own form of Sovereignty and identity. Imagine yourself surrounded with a multitude of "grails of Light" emanating from everything in the space around you. In your heart, acknowledge and give honor to the presence of all these "spines" or "grails" of incarnational and sacred Light.

Imagine your aura of Self-Light—your internal, personal Grail of sacredness and incarnational Light—expanding into the room, joining in love with the myriad multitude of Lights all around you, inviting them into an alliance and collaboration with you. Feel your Light augmenting and blending with the Lights around you, feel their Lights blending with and augmenting your own. You are forming a subtle partnership with your environment and everything seen and unseen within it. Feel this partnership turning your immediate, local environment into a Grail that you and all the things around you collaborate to create, a Grail you share.

The felt sense of this partnership and the field of reciprocal energy that generates it is the Grail Space. It is a field of collaborative partnership and support in the incarnational process with everything around you in your local space, a partnership and fellowship that can receive and hold a Presence of sacredness, a presence of Gaia.

Standing in this Grail Space, acknowledge this Presence of sacredness heightened in yourself and your environment. Imagine it being held in this space, doing whatever it needs to do to foster wholeness and well-being and then overflowing into the larger world beyond, a source of energy, blessing, love, and life.

Stay in this Grail Space as long as feels comfortable. When you feel tired or restless, simply draw your Self-Light back into yourself, giving thanks to your energy partners for their participation. Imagine their incarnational light moving back into themselves as well, knowing the environment you share will resonate with the Light and Presence you have collectively invoked for as long as it is able.

Stand in your Sovereignty, acknowledging your wholeness your integrity, your identity, and your connection to the Sacred. Then go about your daily affairs.

Related Lorian Press Publications

Reflections on the Christ by David Spangler (1978, 2012)

The Unveiled Christos by David Spangler (2005, 2025)

Meditations on Christ by Lee Irwin (2016)

Lorian Press LLC
Coloma, Michigan
lorianpress.etsy.com
lorian.org

www.ingramcontent.com/pod-product-compliance
Lightning Source LLC
Chambersburg PA
CBHW071607170426
43196CB00033B/2141